IT Revolution, Globalization and the Teaching of English

IT Revolution, Globalization and the Teaching of English

Edited by
G. Damodar
P. Shailaja
M. Rajeshwar

ATLANTIC
PUBLISHERS & DISTRIBUTORS (P) LTD

Published by

ATLANTIC

PUBLISHERS & DISTRIBUTORS (P) LTD

B-2, Vishal Enclave, Opp. Rajouri Garden,
New Delhi-110027
Phones : +91-11-25413460, 25429987., 25466842

Sales Office
7/22, Ansari Road, Darya Ganj,
New Delhi-110002
Phones : +91-11-23273880, 23275880, 23280451
Fax : +91-11-23285873
Web : www.atlanticbooks.com
E-mail : info@atlanticbooks.com

Branch Office
5, Nallathambi Street, Wallajah Road,
Chennai-600002
Phones : +91-44-64611085, 32413319
E-mail : chennai@atlanticbooks.com

ISBN 978-81-7156-969-4

Printed in India
at Nice Printing Press, Delhi

PREFACE

The last decade of twentieth century was marked by two dominant phenomena — Information Technology Revolution and Globalization. Both have had profound implications for English language teaching/learning. With the world moving towards Globalization, competent information handling has become vital for survival in a competitive world. The implications of IT revolution for English language teaching are two faceted : firstly, it has led to the shifting of language teaching/learning out of the traditional class-room. In other words, it has facilitated language acquisition through multimedia. Secondly, it has necessitated IT personnel with high communicative competence for its expansion.

IT has been revolutionizing the world and its impact is felt in all walks of life. One cannot think of an area of public life which can do without the use of IT. Computers have become so widespread in schools, colleges and homes and their use has increased so dramatically that the language teachers must now begin to seriously think about the application of computers for imparting language education in a variety of ways. The history of CALL (Computer Assisted Language Learning) suggests that the computer can serve a variety of purposes in language teaching. It can be a tutor offering language drills or skill practice; a stimulus for discussion and interaction; or a tool for writing and research. With the advent of the Internet, it has also become a medium of global communication and a source of limitless authentic materials.

The teachers of English have a special role to play in this context. The learner-centred model is fast replacing the teacher-centred model which has been in vogue for centuries. Hence, there is an imperative need for strengthening the teaching of English by taking stock of its present status and future needs. The computer, used purposefully and innovatively can be an effective tool and enable the teacher to carry out tasks inconceivable by other means.

Yet, it is a mere tool and has no wisdom or mind of its own, no inherent ability to learn or teach. This fact should be never lost sight of. It can never replace the teacher!

It was to address these and other issues that a two-day national seminar was held on 23-24 January 1999 at Kakatiya University, Warangal. The seminar provided a platform for generating discussion on how to incorporate several new concepts into the promotion of quality language education and to support and improve teaching/learning with the help of computers. It focused on the needs of the learners in the changed environment of globalization and stressed the importance of restructuring the syllabi accordingly. The seminar brought together teachers from universities and colleges, counsellors from reputed computer training institutes and representatives of the mass media. The present volume is basically a collection of papers presented at this seminar.

Long ago Coleridge described readers as "hour glasses, strainers, sponges and diamonds." The first category of people read to pass time; the second category miss the flavour of what they read and retain only the dregs; the third category absorb print very effectively and squeeze meaning out of it without noticeable change. It is the last category who are real readers and reflective thinkers. If we substitute the readers with computer users, the hour glasses play arcade and other games, strainers and sponges go through the routine programmes but diamonds use the computer programmes creatively. The present day teachers of English need to be diamonds and make a competent use of computers for instructional purposes.

—Editors

CONTENTS

1
Introduction

P. Shailaja

Information technology (IT) exerts universal appeal in the world of today. It is identified in many countries as perhaps the single most important means to the attainment of economic, social and political ends. Information is that which adds to our awareness or understanding of some topic, problem or event. It is variously perceived as facts, intelligence, data, news and knowledge. It can be print on paper or can come in the form of computer software, electronic mail, videotex and video, compact audio or optical digital disk, etc. Information is the lifeblood of education. It is the essential ingredient in new ideas, in course content and curriculum development, and in the creation of materials and methods for teaching and learning. The new technologies enhance one's ability in the production and dissemination of this educational information, and its management and control.

The term Information technology today is a shifting complex of meanings and interpretations. A simple definition put forward in an exhibition by the Department of Trade and Industry, Great Britain, encompasses information use and content as well as technology itself :

"Information technology is the acquisition, processing, storage, dissemination and use of vocal, pictorial, textual and numerical information by a microelectronics based combination of computing and telecommunications."[1]

Information technology revolution is essentially the product of advances in the three key areas of computing, telecommunications and microelectronics. In fact all the three technologies existed even before. But as it is said, "The whole is greater than the parts," it is their convergence, their coming together that had an effect as radically as did the Industrial revolution on society. Indeed such is their impact and significance, that they are widely regarded as "enabling technologies," the creators of unimaginable possibilities and the facilitators of change. No important field of human endeavour remains immune to its influence and no corner of life is left undisturbed. The social application of these advances resulted in network systems, electronic shopping and banking, business data and government information systems. It gave rise to hopes of an information-rich society. The plain old telephone service is transformed to an image/fax/data/voice network with global connectivity and a gateway to the information superhighway. These innovations led to the development of new interactive media like e-mail (electronic-mail), online information, video conferencing, etc. They have become great facilitators for faster information flow and quicker decision making. To say that these developments have been instrumental in eroding the barriers between nations and reduced the entire globe into a village is not an exaggeration. Coupled with this is the Indian reality of opening up its economy. Indian economy is getting integrated into world economy. Globalisation has become the catch phrase. In this process one needs to interact with people around the world, exchange and share views and negotiate terms. As all this is conveniently done in English, English has acquired a great significance for global communication. English is also used as the international language of IT in general. In fact the relation between English and IT may be described as symbiotic, each benefiting from the other.

The combination of modern IT and Globalization make a formidable force for cultural and educational change. Education is central because electronic networks and software driven technologies are beginning to break down the economic barriers between nations. International communication, which is destined to become extraordinarily cheap in all its forms, will bring suitably educated people from every economic region into the mainstream of the world economy. Well-educated, enterprising individuals with access to IT will do well, no matter where they live.

Hence, all are affected by it and all are challenged not only to adopt new techniques but also to re-think the traditional notions of learning. With the appearance of TVs, computers, video recordings in homes and educational establishments, the nature and content of teaching and learning is changing. At the level of teaching content the teacher's conventional role as provider of knowledge and information is being challenged, while at the level of methodology the way in which the teacher had traditionally related himself with his pupil is challenged. Changes seem to be occurring at all levels and each teacher must respond to and interpret them. There is a pressure for change in classroom management, curricular thinking and educational style.

Education can involve the use of television and radio for the delivery of software and access to courseware written for specific subject areas. It can make use of microcomputers for access to view data and videotex, as well as to on-line databases. It can involve the use of a wide variety of interactive multi-media packages.

The computer has enormous potential as an educational aid providing new language learning opportunities. Used properly it can be very effective enabling the individual to carry out tasks inconceivable by other means. By virtue of its multi-media capacity and its capabilities as a data storage and retrieval system, it may be used very effectively in the learning process. Multi-media technology exemplified today by the CD-ROM allows a variety of media (text, graphics, sound, animation, and video) to be accessed on a single machine.

Hypertext provides a number of advantages for language learning. A more authentic learning environment is created since listening is combined with seeing in the real world. Secondly, skills are easily integrated since the variety of media makes it natural to combine reading, writing, speaking and listening in a simple activity.

There are certain inherent advantages in it. It can handle a much wider range of activities, much more powerfully than other aids. What distinguishes it from others technological aids like Radio, Tape recorders, Overhead projectors is its interactive capability. This means that it can conduct a two-way learning session with the student. To say in the words of Nelson,

"The unique property of the computer as a medium for education is its ability to interact with the student. Books and tape recordings can tell a student what the rules are and what the right solutions are, but they cannot analyze the specific mistake the student had made and react in a manner which leads him not only to correct his mistake, but also to understand the principles behind the correct solutions."

The computer offers certain advantages for the learner : it has a number of advantages over normal classwork. It offers privacy and allows learners to work on their own, in their own time at their own pace, thus catering to the needs of both slow and fast learners. It is patient and will tirelessly go over the same points for as long as is necessary. Each response of the learner receives a reply from the computer, immediately with appropriate feedback in the form of comments, assessment and guidance. It generally adapts the material to the learner's performance, and allows him to choose from several modes of presentation.

The computer thus promotes the acquisition of knowledge at the learner's own pace, demands active participation and develops his critical faculties.

Above all, the computer holds a fascination, particularly for the young. This may partly be due to the visual effects afforded by the system or because of the novelty of working with the computer. Many had been introduced to computers through games and they probably think using a computer to be fun. As a result of this unique combination of interactive, tutorial and visual capabilities, computers frequently have a beneficial effect on learner motivation.

The computer has obvious advantages for the teacher: Computer can be an effective tool, and like any other electronic or electric gadget, provides a means of amplifying or extending the effectiveness of teachers natural talents and capabilities. It offers him an opportunity to deal with large classes effectively.

The simplest task a computer performs is the one-way presentation of information in the form of text, graphics, audio and video. It can handle question and answer routines, simulated dialogues, hypothesis testing, and many other types of exercise. It can record results, errors and success rate, time spent and any other information for the teacher to view at a later time. By taking over these tedious mechanical tasks, it allows him to spend more time on preparation and on activities such as discussion. The feedback enables a teacher to evaluate the materials, refine, revise and modify unlike the present.

Researchers in recent years seem to be more and more convinced that language teaching and learning is more effective if the curriculum is styled to suit the learner needs, and if the learners are given greater responsibility for their learning process. Discovery learning, that is, the formation and testing of hypothesis becomes a basic strategy in acquiring competence in a language other than the mother tongue. An environment, which provides ample material and freedom for this type of discovery learning, is hard to create in a traditional classroom. But a computer offers this unique opportunity for the learner.

The software used for language learning mostly include the following exercise patterns in their programmes.

Drill and Practice : This is the most common type of exercise, but is relevant even today. In the most basic programmes, the learner chooses a grammar point or vocabulary lesson. The computer asks a question and the learner responds. If the answer is correct the programme moves on to the next question. The main advantage of simple drills is that many students who need repeated practice on vocabulary or grammatical concepts benefit from entering their answers and receiving immediate feedback.

There are more complex programmes, which analyze the answer and give specific feedback as to the nature of the error and direct the learner to a review section. The most sophisticated ones use branching strategies to lead the learner through remedial exercises until a specific concept is mastered and then returns him to the main programme.

Simulations : A learner uses language in simulations, which try to imitate real life experiences. Some of the interesting features of the computer are used to supply basic information that the learner develops further in writing.

A very common simulation programme is of a student arriving at a U.S. airport. The student must go through customs, find transportation to the city, and check in at a hotel. The language learner using the program assumes the role of the arriving student by interacting with simulated people who appear in video clips and responding to what they say by typing in responses. If the responses are correct, the student is sent off to do other things, such as meeting a roommate. If the responses are incorrect, the program takes remedial action by showing examples or breaking down the task into smaller parts. At any time the student can control the situation by asking what to do, what to say, asking to hear again what was just said, requesting for a translation, or controlling the level of difficulty of the lesson.

Games are also examples of simulation programmes. The learner plays a role during which he makes decisions, solves problems and learns by his mistakes. The English teacher's interest lies in the learners working towards the goals entirely through language use.

Word-processors : To date the best language related use is still word-processing. It provides powerful facilities for both creating and editing or correcting texts, letters, words and sentences. Paragraphs can be overwritten, inserted, moved, copied or deleted anywhere in a text. The changes can then be inspected on the screen, before a final version is decided on. Experiments with using word processing in composition classes have shown that this tends to encourage them to write more and edit more.

Internet and *e-mail* provide an opportunity for authentic language interaction and learning. E-mail can be used to send short, personal, conversational messages, letters etc. by the users. It thus facilitates interaction with others and helps learn English in a real life situation. The world wide web is a great resource and presents information in layers.

To sum up, the advantages in using these technological manifestations include : exposure to new ideas and experiences; development of logical thinking and reasoning abilities; support for training in skills or for remedial activity and the simulation of real life situations.

However, there are some genuine problems in using the computer for language teaching. Firstly this technology mediated system is expensive and an access to the equipment is denied even to most of the teachers. Secondly an equally serious problem is, education through computers depends on high quality software and courseware which is not yet available. The development of CALL programmes requires knowledge of three fields : competence in the target subject area, pedagogical skill and computing expertise. A single individual cannot be well-versed in all these skills. Hence, the courseware available so far for use is inadequate in quality, quantity and variety.

But if one can get over these problems, which certainly can happen in future, the computer can become the most powerful aid in this technology driven age and an answer to the over-crowded language classes.

As stated in an old Chinese saying a learner learns best through seeing and doing :

Tell a child something and he forgets it
Show a child something and he remembers it
Let a child do something and he knows it.[2]

So, rather than being the recipients of mere information, if a learner is given an opportunity to engage himself in meaningful activities involving language use, it would be more useful. What the computer technology offers is a resource, which helps the teacher accomplish classroom changes, which are long overdue.

The present volume focuses on the challenges faced by the Indian teachers of English in the changed context of Globalisation and Information Technology revolution, and the application of IT to support and improve the teaching/learning situation.

Notes and References

1. Quoted by William J. Martin, *The Information Society* (London : Aslib, 1988) 24.
2. George R. Keith and Malcolm Glover, *Primary Language Learning with Microcomputers* (London : Croom Helm, 1987) 9.

2

Information Technology Revolution: Opportunities and Challenges to the Teachers of English

M. Rajeshwar

> The English language brings to every student, as no Indian language can at the present moment, the latest information from every part of the world. In our historical situation we owe this to English. In this sense the English teacher is by definition an agent of technological progress, of cultural awakening, and of international understanding.
>
> K. Ayyappa Paniker, "English Studies in India," *Littcrit* 23 (June-Dec. 1997): 35.

The Information Technology Revolution, made possible through the introduction of computers in every field of human activity, has completely altered our approach to life. For teachers and educators the computer has opened up profound new possibilities to impart language education. The introduction of the computer into the language classroom as a resource adds to the excitement and ease of teaching and learning. The multi-media computer simultaneously appeals to the senses of seeing and hearing in a way traditional teaching aids cannot; it reinforces and supports the learning strategies the student evolves for himself rather than coerce him to adapt to new strategies which are alien to his nature. It offers a high degree of flexibility in learning. The student can sit with a computer whenever he likes and as long as he likes. It never objects to anything. It teaches him at a pace at which he feels comfortable.

The difficulty experienced by slow learners in a conventional classroom is easily eliminated.

The name given to computer enhanced classroom environment is called "Computer Assisted Language Learning" (CALL). CALL programs make use of software specially developed for the purpose of second language acquisition and instruction and make the teaching and learning of English an infinitely enjoyable experience.[1] These programs are so designed as to respect the individuality of the student by giving him a number of options and by never frowning at him when he makes mistakes. He therefore feels relaxed and is not worried about being corrected, judged or watched. There is considerable amount of novelty and excitement in these programs. They are interactive and user friendly. A wrong answer entered by the student, for example, immediately draws forth the correct version, which apart from helping him to learn what is right also enables him to evaluate his own performance on the spot. They present even intricate points of grammar and language skills through games and problem-solving techniques. Where necessary, sound and color effects can be added to the text. Hypertext items are a great source of further information about intricate points of language. The serious student who has a mind to probe these depths gets the satisfaction of solving a mystery. In the last analysis, any student learning English with the help of CALL programs ends up feeling that he is playing a game or solving a problem when actually he is learning.

The Internet too has thrown up exciting new possibilities and opportunities to teachers and learners of English. The e-mail which is part of the Internet and which is offered freely by many portals such as Yahoo.com, Excite.com, etc.,[2] can be used as a great means of composition exercise in letter-writing. The teacher should first establish contact with a like minded teacher in another country, preferably an English speaking country, and encourage his class of students to write e-mail letters to, become e-friends so to say of, the students of his contact. These letters should be closely supervised and sometimes read out in the classroom at both ends. It is now possible to send multi-media e-mail or voice-mail too. This mode of e-mail allows recorded voice to accompany the text. Lucent Voice Player (LVP), which is a small utility, makes it possible to compress a voice file to 1/5th of its size so that a large file can be transferred easily. Listening to the recorded voices of the students and teachers of a foreign nation can help in getting exposed to different accents of English. Thus apart from offering fun and excitement the e-mail can facilitate easy interaction with English speaking students outside the country and help learn English in a real life situation and all this very fast and at no great cost.

Similarly the World Wide Web (WWW), the jewel of the Internet, comes as a great resource for language learning and teaching and can be used effectively in the language classroom. The WWW is littered with websites specializing in classroom materials, lesson plans, course descriptions, bibliographies, class activities, etc.[3] A meaningful attribute of it is the hypertext which presents information in layers. As has been said earlier on, with the help of hypertext it is possible to read a text at varying degrees of complexity and depth and if a dictionary is "embedded" (in-built), as in Microsoft Bookshelf Basics, the mystery of difficult and unfamiliar words can be solved at the click of the mouse button. Another very useful application of the Web, one which has great value for the teaching/learning of English, is video-conferencing. By means of a special video camera, a sound card and network connectivity teachers and students of one country can now interact live with their counterparts in another and learn many things from each other about language related issues. Even lectures delivered by experts at one place can be heard and viewed everywhere in the world, all for a farthing. Another mode of live interaction on the net is the Chat site.[4] This is a real-time conversation facility, until recently only text based but now audio is being increasingly added. The learners of English can use the Chat sites in a variety of ways. By becoming regular chatters, they can learn to express themselves very fast in meaningful English sentence. They can acquire a wealth of current idioms, phrases and expressions from their chat partners because the chat language tends to be informal and colloquial. The Web has thus provided both the teachers and learners an opportunity for authentic language interaction and learning.

It may be added here that it is not just the computer alone which has interactive applications. Even the good old TV (now sought to be rechristened "Smart TV" or "Internet TV") is fast assuming interactive capabilities with the help of TC 701 technology of

TeleCruz. It will be soon possible to log on to the Internet without the complexity of the computer and in a cost-effective way. In other words, students can use the Internet without unduly worried about the costs and in the comfort of their living rooms.[5]

There is nothing fanciful about what I have been saying all this while. Computers and Internet are the realities of today and they are here to stay. In Andhra Pradesh, for instance, computers are fast becoming a household necessity. Most educated people already own them. At the level of the administration, the process of joining all district headquarters by a computer network is afoot. This network is intended to facilitate video-conferencing, electronic file transfer and data collaboration. It is also proposed to establish electronic kiosks all over the state to keep information about government orders and programs, movement of files, the timings of buses and trains, etc., readily available to the people. The future belongs to the computers and computer literacy and Internet fluency will be of great advantage to everybody. The one language which helps us to acquire these skills and use computers to the maximum advantage is English and the recognition of this fact has profound implications in terms of language policy planning and poses equally profound challenges to the teachers of English. The English teachers have to adapt to the new technology to maximize their teaching potential. They should readjust their thinking to face this challenge on its own terms and without entertaining any misgivings. They should not be afraid that the computer would become some kind of a surrogate teacher or replace them altogether.[6] Far from that, the technology enhanced classroom environment will make teaching language a challenging and exciting enterprise. Although many CALL programs, and Computer Based Teaching (CBT) programs, have the emergence of the autonomous learner as one of the aims, it is never an easy possibility. The teacher will remain indispensable. In fact, his responsibilities will multiply. He should not, for example, be satisfied with the commercial software but design his own materials which are compatible with CALL even for his teacher-led classes and develop computer-oriented tasks for stimulating language learning.

Unfortunately, however, the Indian teachers of English are at present hardly equipped to match these expectations. English is generally not taught by people who are well qualified to teach it by training or aptitude. At the school level, while there are trained pundits to teach Indian languages, any Bachelor of Education can teach English.[7] Not surprisingly therefore the largest percentage of failures in the school final (SSC) examination are in English. At college, in most cases, the lecturers have no formal training at all to teach English. Training is not an entry-level requirement for a lecturer. The net result of all this is that the average Indian student, in spite of about ten years of exposure to English, fails to acquire the much needed receptive and productive skills. This is a sad commentary on the history of English teaching in India and the situation can be improved only when the teaching of English is thoroughly professionalized and teachers are trained and made accountable.

Professionalizing the teaching of English involves training the teachers right from the plus two level, almost the same way as we train our doctors and lawyers to become what they are from the point of entering the college. The ideal syllabus for this five-year degree course should include grammar, phonetics, English linguistics, literature, psychology, pedagogy and computer science. Further, English should be treated as an Indian language and it should be learnt for its use value in the changed scenario of the IT revolution and globalization and not because of its prestige or sentimental value. This change in attitude will enable us to look upon the language as a skill to be acquired for ensuring success in life. The teachers of English should help bring about this transition by gearing themselves up to face the new challenges and the policy planners, apart from insisting on teacher training in English, should give the teachers, where they need, the freedom to design their own courses and administer them the way they like, subject to their delivering goods.

Notes and References

1. Some of the famous CALL programs now available are: Text Mixer, Wordstore, Storyboard, Pinpoint, Test Master, Match Master, Gap Master, Grammar Focus Advanced, Vocab Focus Advanced 1-2, Exam Focus Prof Discs 1-2 and Exam Focus FCE Discs 1-3.

2. Here is a list of sites offering free Web-based e-mail accounts :
   http://www.hotmail.com
   http://www.starmail.com
   http://www.juno.com
   http://www.indiamail.com
   http://www. mail.excite.com
   http://www.mailcity lycos.com
   http://www.netaddress.com
   http://www.pobox.com
   http://www.rocketmail.com
3. There are hundreds of websites offering programs in English, ELT and related areas. These can be accessed, and in most cases downloaded, with the help of any search engine.
4. Some popular chat sites are :
   www.talkcity.com
   www.webnautics.com
   www.virtual-media.com
   www.4-lane.com
   www.frontiernet.net
   www.globalmatch.com
   www.theglobe.com
   www.folksoline.com
   www.excite.com
5. Even as we talk about the Internet TV, the consumer electronics company BPL has already introduced it in the Indian market.
6. The students themselves do not seem to favour the idea of computers replacing the teachers. According to a recent survey conducted by the daily *Deccan Chronicle* (22 Feb. 1999), 77% of students have indicated their preference for teachers over computers, but felt that the computer could be the most useful teaching aid.
7. I understand that the AP Government has recently declared its intention to create the post of School Assistant in English. It is indeed a welcome step and well worthy of emulation.

3

Damu CALL in English

G. Damodar

Introduction

First, a brief review of Computer Assisted Instruction (CAI) in English is presented. Making an appraisal of Computer Assisted Language Learning (CALL) programs, it is shown how microcomputers have become convenient tools for researchers in language studies and how Computer Video Combination (CVC) has an advantage over the ordinary CALL programs. Finally, some programs, titled Damu CALL Programs, are suggested for non-native learners of English.

Computer Assisted Instruction (CAI)

The possibilities of classroom applications and research in language studies with the help of PCs are immense now. Now the PCs have become the attractive teaching and learning aids of English and the most convenient tools in the hands of teachers and researchers of language studies. They can be used as a substitute as well as an aid to the teacher for classroom instruction. Advanced study centres in India like Central Institute of English and Foreign Languages (CIEFL), Centre for Applied Linguistics of University of Hyderabad and Some IITs and RECs have already experienced the integration of the PCs into research and instruction. The technological background of data driven learning has been on the increase in these five years in storage capacity and processing speed of affordable microcomputers. Progress has been made to the point that small, inexpensive computers with expanded capabilities are available for innumerable uses.

Most scholars now agree that the microcomputers have changed our attitude to teaching and research. While Gubser (1980) and Hinton (1980) visualized a phenomenal growth in computer education, Schmidt (1982) identified three types of microcomputer applications in instruction: the object of a cause, a support tool and a means of providing instruction. Foster and Kleen (1982) refer to four uses of microcomputers in vocational training: drill and practice, tutorial, simulation and problem solving. Studies by Hickey (1968) and Honeycutt (1974) showed superior results with Computer Assisted Instruction (CAI), while studies by Ellis (1978), Caldwell (1980) and Belzer (1976) showed little effect of CAI.

Although much work has been done to data abroad, serious studies need to be conducted to ascertain the effects of CAI programs in a variety of learning situations where English is learnt and taught as a second and foreign language. Of late, interactive CAI programs are being advocated as the most versatile aids for individualized instruction and learning (Lalit 1989).

Appraisal of CALL Programs

Roger Stank, America's leading figure in the field of Artificial Intelligence (AI), covers the hopes that have been voiced by a section of the teaching community as a consequence of the computer revolution: computers are fun; they can be programed to teach far more thoroughly and interactively than text-books; they serve as excellent individualized teachers. A student can have his own computer teacher who keeps track of progress; these computer teachers can be used by almost anyone, no matter how lazy or hyperactive; they do not get bored or frustrated with students or with teaching; they will not punish the student or single him out for contempt. Even timid students who are often afraid of making fools of themselves in the classroom are comfortable with the computers. Games were not only among the first programs to appear on the PC software market; they were also among the first productions of AI researchers interested in problem solving. That was because the rules and elements of games constitute finite sets and thus proved relatively easy to devise a program. Games are fun, whether played on computers or otherwise. Since they are the most popular types of software, many of us identify games with PCs. This however does not guarantee that every kind of interaction with computers is fun and exciting. In fact, much of the current teaching software is a source of frustration for the student-user in that communication with the machine is often awkward (Nievergelt, *et al.,* 1986).

Most CALL programs still consist of rather tedious drill activities, close-type exercises or multiple-choice questionnaires. These activities stand in strong contrast to the generally accepted concept of communicative teaching, which sheds light on the limits and perils of repetitive drills in language learning and teaching. Those programs which do allow for creativity and initiative on the students' behalf have a very restricted domain of discourse connotating that they model part of a complex system which has been arbitrarily reduced to a finite set of objects, as for example in Higgins (1985) "Grammarland" program and Broderbund Software's "Where in the World is Carmen Sandiego?" Students and teachers, who lack the necessary typing skills to work at a reasonable pace, do not enjoy interaction with the computers. Some are apprehensive about what the machine does with their input (keeping tracking of their mistakes!). They miss the warmth of human interaction. Many students still prefer human teachers who very often get bored and irritated to inanimate machines which are infallible and stick to the pre-programed tasks.

Nevertheless, microcomputers can be programed to teach more thoroughly and interactively than textbooks. Whereas books are regarded as one medium at the teacher's disposal along with some aids, the PCs are now very often viewed as surrogate teachers. No doubt, Multimedia PCs can do things no other media can, such as imparting effective instruction through text, sound and graphics, keeping track of students' progress, choosing grades of difficulty and providing immediate feedback to the students' responses to exercises and the like. To this extent, they can take over a major part of the teaching process, which has been so far done manually by teachers.

For Research in Language Studies

In the field of language studies, Concordance Software is a convenient tool for English linguists. Concordance is a program that is able to search rapidly through several pages of a text for a target item, say a morpheme, a word or a phrase, and print out all the examples it finds with the contexts in which they appear. Items typed in the irregular order can also be arranged in an alphabetical manner in no time. Multifarious kinds of corpus (huge chunks of language texts) have been developed in Concordance for uncovering several language truths.

The increased availability of ready-made corpora of machine-readable text and the possibilities of automatic entry of corpora through scanners and Optical Character Recognition (OCR) Software has been an added advantage to the lexicographers, text-book writers and education planners. Now researchers with the help of Concordance can study a particular linguist element — word, morpheme or phrase — used in all the contexts. Some of the Concordance programs are Tim John's MICROCONCORD, OCP Package from OUP, WORD-CRUNCHER from Brimgham University, Joseph Roseau's CONCORDTEACH and the Longmans MINI-CONCORDANCER. COBUILD Dictionary is the outcome of the influence in database in looking at the way the word in particular and the language in general functions.

CALL Programs Abroad

Some of the programs of CALL software available abroad include :

1. Adventures in Speaking English
2. Choice Master
3. Exam Focus
4. TOFEL Practice Disk
5. GRE CD ROM
6. Gapmaster
7. Grammar Focus Advanced
8. Match Master
9. Pinpoint
10. Storyboard
11. Test Master
12. Text Mixer
13. Topic Focus

14. Vocabulary Focus Advanced 1 & 2
15. Wordstore
16. Wordcruncher
17. Wordsmith
18. ProQuest
19. Grammar
20. Vocabulary

Most of the above modules, though not curriculum-oriented, are indeed versatile and user-friendly. They are primarily aimed at different native learners of English. Several items needed for second and foreign language learners are ignored in these modules. For example, in the first one titled "Adventures in Speaking English," developed by Jiva Institute in 1998 for ages 10 and up, is an animated adventure based on some proven teaching methods with over sixty quicktime movies for original animation. It runs for two hours with record and playback facilities. It has lip-synchronised voice-overs with dazzling graphics for some practice in vowel and sibilant sounds, stops and continuing sounds, pitch, blending, word and sentence rhythm, etc., in R.P., which is a hard nut to crack for several non-native speakers of English. A professor goes to Uvula, a remote island in South Africa and gets involved, as a witness, to the witch-doctor's secret attempt to steal the diamond eyes of the village God. Cursed by the witch and held captive by the natives, the professor barely manages to call his secretary JJ in New York. JJ calls in the international team of adventures led by Murray A Pockapee to locate the Professor. The team starts its investigation, but gets invariably stuck at obstacles that only of this CD-ROM can resolve by taking the English lessons and giving the correct responses. This intriguing storyline indeed makes learning fun as *computer@home* rightly says. It adopts objective-type-problem-solving methodology. It is based on active learning methodology and helps the users to improve their spoken English. It follows context-based but not text-based approach, which might pose a problem to some non-native learners of English. Moreover, it requires IBM PC compatible with 486 DX2 processor, mouse, 8MB RAM, 16 bit sound blaster, microphone, SVGA 256 colors or higher with 640X480 display, Windows 95 which are not available with several users. The eighteenth one, titled ProQuest, is a self-contained computer program, a search engine, for UMI-produced CDs. It is only available for a DOS environment, *i.e.*, not Windows or Mac. The SU library version runs it on a dedicated PC which automatically takes the user directly into ProQuest. At each step along the way, there are help screens available. The users are not given access to the operating system of PC, although they will be able to download material onto floppies. The major limitation of ProQuest is linguistic : it will not search for primarily prepositions and function words as they have low content value for information retrieval. Investigations of items like the, this, their, on, at, under, all, etc., and patterns such as arrive at or arrive in some place, good at or good in something, etc., really require access to another program such as Wordcruncher or Wordsmith.

Hence, there is an imperative need now to modify and adopt these programs to the situations of non-native learners of English.

Damu CALL Programs for Non-Native Learners

Damu CALL Programs devised by the author me include twenty-six modules on all the important aspects of English usage which non-native learners of English need for various purposes. They include :

1. Language Functions 1 — to identify the forms of sentences
2. Language Functions 2 — to improve your communicative power
3. Verb Paradigms — to know about five forms of verbs
4. Missing Letters — to test your spelling power
5. Word Endings — to choose between two choices
6. Right Words — to select the appropriate word
7. Misspelt Words — to find the words with wrong spelling
8. Gender — to learn masculine and feminine nouns
9. Pronunciation — to identify the similar sounds in words
10. Prepositions — to select the proper preposition
11. Antonyms — to suggest words of opposite meaning
12. Punctuation Pointers — to use proper signs and marks in writing
13. Tenses — to frame the sentences in twelve tense forms
14. Synonyms — to guess the words of similar meaning

15.	Jumbled Letters	—	to rearrange the letters in correct order
16.	Our Parts of Speech	—	to form nouns, adjectives, verbs and adverbs
17.	Single Word Substitution	—	to substitute a group of words with a single word
18.	Articles	—	to use appropriate articles
19.	Question Tags	—	to frame suitable tag questions
20.	Passivization	—	to convert the voice of the sentences
21.	Single or Double	—	to separate the double words
22.	Jumbled Words	—	to arrange the words for meaningful sentences
23.	Shuffled Sentences	—	to arrange the sentences for proper paragraphs
24.	Singular/Plural	—	to guess the singular and the plural words
25.	Synthesis of Sentences	—	to combine sentences with 'so...that' and 'too...to'
26.	Detection of Errors	—	to detect the misused part of the sentence
	Exit	—	to end the program and see your performance report.

Most of these tasks are given for testing at different levels in a conventional mode over the decades at Bhavan Institute of English (BIE), Hanamkonda, with or without the help of computers. The modules have been written in Pascal language in about 5,000 lines of code and have been updated periodically based on the feedback. The following are the features of the package :

1. It is a randomized package, *i.e.* the questions are selected at random. The users never get the same set of questions whenever they start their practice. The answers go on shuffling from time to time avoiding monotony.
2. Number of attempts is unlimited in each module. Additions and deletions can be done effortlessly with a simple text-editor and a single command.
3. Some help is also provided before a particular item starts.
4. Boosters such as Good answer, Nice answer, Well done, That's great, Fantastic, Fabulous, You got it, Fine, Excellent, Marvellous, That's fine, Keep it up, You are right, You are great, You are correct, You are bright,

You are intelligent, You've got the point, You've got the right answer, Absolutely correct, Quite correct, Quite OK, Yes, Yes, Yes, That's wonderful, Yeah, You are great, I appreciate you for this, That's it, There you are, Good guess, That's excellent, That's marvellous, That's fantastic, That's splendid, etc., are used with a sweet chirping tune to encourage the practising students.

5. When wrong answers are given, the correct ones appear with an alerting tune.
6. Suitable solutions are supplied if the wrong answers are suggested.
7. Module 7 first congratulates the student on selecting the right number of the misspelt word and then asks him to type in the correct spelling giving him enough practice in typing.
8. Instant scoring is displayed at the top right-hand corner of the screen and it is automatically recorded for self-evaluation. There is continuous monitoring and testing of the performance of students.
9. The Program concludes with Performance Report of the students with the modules practised, items attempted, number of correct attempts with percentage. It also shows whether the performance is poor, average, good or excellent.
10. The package is suitable for Indian environment in tune with the systems available. Several schools and colleges, where the present package is useful, have old PC 286 or 386 machines.
11. The package can also be downloaded onto any floppy or hard disk. It can be easily installed and run on any PC ranging from XT to Pentiums with DOS or WINDOWS Operating System.
12. Similar Window-based packages use at least 5 MB of disk space and need 5 floppies. They require latest machines with multimedia facilities. But the present package takes only 0.5 MB space.

13. Any student with a sound knowledge of PASCAL or C language can devise such packages.
14. Study Material has also been prepared as a companion to the modules for reinforcement and extensive reading.
15. It is a menu-driven package as opposed to a character-interface of 80s which displays only options. It is very user-friendly.
16. Version 2.2 will be an improvement over 1.95 as Multi-media package with more items, images, sounds, animations and video clippings for the latest multi-media computers and internet browsers. It is under development and testing at BIE.

The needs of the students are taken into consideration while deciding the contents of the CALL programs. At secondary school level in Andhra Pradesh, the students are asked to identify the expressions of greetings, requests, orders, permissions, suggestions, questions, wishes, regrets, etc., in a multiple-choice pattern. In this conventional written examination, the students have to select the appropriate answer and write its number in the space provided. In CALL programs, if a wrong answer is given, the computer shows the correct answer. Immediate correction and remediation is possible with a computer unlike the traditional question paper.

Most of the students of English in India go wrong when they use verb paradigms. They are not aware of the rules of adding "-s" or "-es" to the verb in singular for third person (such as allot-allots; go-goes; cry-cries; buy-buys) and "-ing" to the verb in present participle. They should know that "-es" is added to the verbs ending in "o", "x", "ss", "sh", "ch" and when "y" becomes "i" (as in do-does; fax-faxes; pass-passes; wash-washes; latch-latches; try-tries; etc). While adding "-ing" the verb undergoes certain changes. If the last letter is preceded by a single vowel, the last letter is doubled as in ban-banning; step-stepping; stop-stopping; begin-beginnig; cut-cutting, etc. If there are two vowels at a time or more than two vowels at different places and if the verbs end in "w", "x", or "y", the last letter is not doubled as in beat-beating, draw-drawing; xerox-xeroxing; pay-paying; etc. The module on verb paradigms explains these rules with examples at the beginning and tests eight hundred verbs in five forms in different order for different students with their scoring online.

The module on Tenses gives a detailed information regarding the uses of twelve tenses, which are indeed confusing for Indian learners of English. It presents all the tenses in the form of a chart at a glance for easy and quick learning. A sample verb "go" is used in all its forms and tenses in linear and horizontal way. In the module, students are encouraged to use some important transitive verbs like allot, begin, break, buy, choose, do, drink, eat, give, know, make, meet, pay, speak, take, teach, tell, wear, write, etc., as explained in the chart in twelve tense forms. When all these are shown at a glance on the monitor, the students will have a total understanding of tenses as opposed to page-wise information which they tend to forget when they proceed to the next page.

In the context of reading, flexibility expresses the need for different modes of reading, adapted to various types of text and goals in reading them. For example, one reads an abstract in an academic journal one way and an article in *The Indian Express* in another. This is to some extent related to reading speed control, as skim reading of certain texts can be "forced." Highlighting a text and focusing on logical connectors will also develop this important skill. This can be achieved using printed matter and more vividly over-head projector, but the microcomputer allows the combination of visual display with time control and can do this individually for each student.

Some of the modules are open-ended while many of them are closed. In the modules on Tenses, Passivization, Antonyms and Languages Functions, which are primarily meant for communication, students have the choice for open-ended responses. For example, your friend has started watching late night movies on Cable TV. You think he is neglecting his studies. Advise him not to do it. Your responses might be

(a) If I were you, I would avoid watching all those programs.

(b) I advise you not to neglect your studies.

(c) Don't neglect your studies.

(d) Hope you will not mind if I ask you not to waste your time.

(e) I wish you could be more serious about studies.

(f) Had I been in your place, I would not have watched them.

(g) Watching late night movies disturbs you.

(h) What you need now is sound knowledge of your subject, but not late night movies.

(i) Be serious about your studies, etc.

Students have freedom to frame their own expressions. If their response does not match with the programed responses, all the correct choices will appear on the screen for their extensive learning. The disadvantage of this module is that it may not accept even the correct answer other than the preprogramed ones. Nevertheless, it suggests some more relevant answers.

Computer Video Combination (CVC)

Recently, computer controlled videos through an interface have been developed to overcome some limitations of CALL floppies. Another name for the video-computer interface system is "Interactive Video" (IV) as it can interact with the viewer and provide an ideal tool to make the teaching-learning process both efficient and effective. It is treated as the convergence of all media.

CVC is an effective tool to reinforce certain components of curriculum in a lively manner. Students can assess their spoken English and judge their gestures. They can pick up correct sentences in appropriate situations by watching video lessons produced by BBC such as "On We Go," "Person to Person," etc. CVC combines the advantages, of both the computer and the motion pictures. This type of combination is said to be the most versatile teaching aid and it is likely to revolutionize the classroom instruction in near future.

The IV instruction is a method of interaction with the facility of random accessibility of a very large textual visual and audio database. This system of instruction can provide individualized reinforcement and feedback in a predetermined form for each learner.

A video disc as a storage and play back medium offers a number of advantages. It has a large storage capacity. A 30 cm diameter video disc can cover over a thousand still pictures, slides, textbook pages, 20 hours of audio recording and two hours of audio-visual motion material. It has a high storage flexibility. On a video disc any combination of audio-visual material can be stored as per the needs of individual students. It is a quick random access system. The video disc rotates very fast and a light beam stylus lifts the information for display on the monitor of a computer. Forward and backward movements, and to and fro movements of stylus make branching operations easy. As the videodisc is made of a strong plastic material, it is robust and lasting. Also wear and tear of the disc is negligible as there is no physical contact between the stylus and the disc. The videodisc can be played at fast and slow motions and the frames can also be freezed. Multiple audio tracks in a videodisc can be used for students with different mother tongues. It can be extremely useful in India in which instruction is given in different regional languages. Finally, it can make classroom instruction individualized. The facility branching on a videodisc can provide instruction for slow, average and bright students.

Video Disc System of Instruction

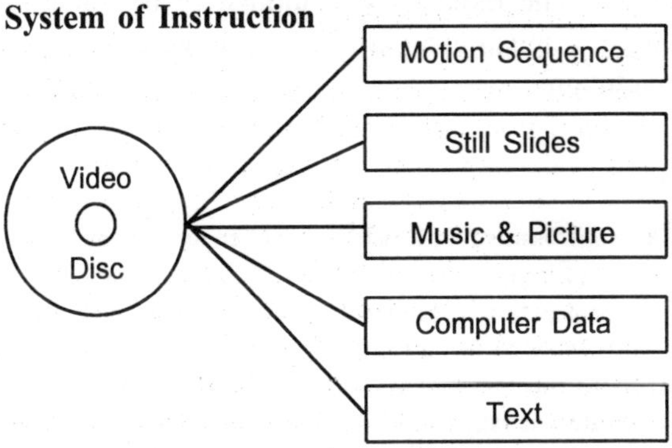

The videodisc and computer interface has a lot of educational implications. Apart from the usual CAI formats for testing tutorials and practice, it has the following additional applications : it can simulate situations for effective teaching and learning of English. It can simulate social and human interactions to optimize instructional outcomes. It can teach in a standardized and perfect way any aspect of an instructional segment. It can store a large amount of audio-visual database from various book and non-book sources. It can store and compare visual material for art, craft, acting and other performance training. It can help in adapting learning material for students of different abilities. It can have universal use by multiple audio-tracks of flexibility.

There is a great potential of Interactive Video for individualizing the classroom teaching in future. The new microcomputer revolution which Artificial Intelligence represents is still marching and it has a bright future before robot teachers walk into the classroom.

Conclusion

The programs presented here are still under research and development. The author wants to devise different versions of CALL programs for different target groups using text, sound and graphics in a self-instructional format. Some modules then will cover communicative English as Cook (1988) hoped, in a variety of situations that are likely to be encountered by the non-native learners of English. The modules will ultimately be aimed at teacherless teaching of English in an effective and interesting way in the era of IT Revolution.

Notes

1. The word 'assisted' in CALL is very often replaced by 'aided'.
2. Since we belong to the fourth generation of computers, the term "microcomputers" (Multimedia PCs) is used for pedagogical purposes and "supercomputers" for scientific applications.
3. Artificial Intelligence (AI) is the study of computer problem-solving tasks which are generally considered proper to human intelligence.
4. "Computer-mediated Combination" is modified here as "Computer Video Combination" (CVC) which is also called "Interactive Video" (IV).
5. "Simulation" refers to real life situations in which the students need not take any active part.
6. This CD-ROM, which costs about Rs. 650, can be had from Cyber Multimedia, D-126, Panchsheel Enclave, New Delhi 110017. Phone: 6433999/6471320. Fax: 011-6475765. E-mail: cybermm@cmil.com.
7. From the research done by Mr. David Minugh, Department of English, Stockholm University, Sweden.
8. In a phased manner, these CALL programs will be designed separately for schools as CALL for Schools covering the topics given for testing in final examination; for colleges as CALL for Colleges with prescribed exercises of

grammar and composition, for computer students as CALL for Computer Students covering the topics of communicative English; for competitive aspirants as CALL for Competitive Aspirants with tasks covered in several competitive examinations; for usage as CALL for Usage covering a thousand sentences for correct usage; and for Communication as CALL for Communication suggesting the different ways to improve communicative skills.

9. I thank Mr. V. Narender, the main program writer, Mr. G. Srinivas, Mr. M. Naveen, and Ms. Yasmin D. Mandani for their constant assistance in my CALL programs.

Works Cited

Belzer, TU. 1976. "A Comparative Study of a Traditional Lecture Method and a Group-paced, Multimedia, Non-Lecture Method." ERIC Document Reproduction Service No. ED 133026.

Brodarbund Software. 1985. "Where in the World is Carmen Sandeigo?"

Caldwell, RM. 1980. "A Comparision of using Computer-based Education to Teach Literacy and Numeracy Skills to CETA and non-CETA students." ERIC DRS No. ED 194721.

Cook, VJ. 1988. "Designing Call Programs for Communicative Teaching." *ELT Journal* 244 : 262-71.

Foster, R. and M. Kleen. 1982. "Opportunities with Computer Assisted Instruction." *The Education Magazine* 54.7 : 12-14.

Gubser, L. 1980. "Schools of Education—a Time for Revolution." ERIC DRS No. ED 195-524.

Hickey, A.E. 1968. "Computer Assisted Instruction : A Survey of the Literature." Newburyport, MA : ENTELEK.

Hinton, Jr. 1980. "Individualized Learning Using Micro-Computer CAI." ERIC DRS No. ED 196409.

Honneycut, Jr. 1974. "The Effects of Computer Managed Instruction on Content Learning of Undergraduate Students." ERIC DRS No. ED 089682.

Lalit, K. 1989. *A Textbook of Audio-Visual Aids.* Delhi : Doaba House.

Neivergelt, *et al.* 1986. *Interactive Computer Programming for Education.* Reading, Mass : Addison-Wesley.

Philips, M. 1986. "CALL in its Educational Context." *Computers in ELT and Research* ed. Leech and Candlin. London : Longman.

Schmidt, Jr. 1982. "Computer Utilization of Resident Instruction at the Land Grant University (UM)." North Central Computer Institute, Madison.

4

Globalization, English Teaching and Information Technology

P. Dhanavel

Introduction

English in India is as old as the East India Company. It rose to prominence with the emergence of the British Raj and got fully institutionalized in the educational sector in 1857 when the first three universities were established in Calcutta, Bombay and Madras. The position of English remained unaltered until the Indian Independence in 1947. Then English became an Associate Official Language. Hindi and other national languages came to be promoted fervently. It was believed by the national leaders that English would gradually be replaced in every sphere of life, including administration, education and mass media. However, the language has continued to hold its spell over the people. There have always been demands for more of English medium schools and colleges. Now that globalization and information technology have come to stay and strengthen, English is drawing attention to itself afresh as a language worth learning for the abundant opportunities it provides for the individual growth and development.

Globalization

The concept of "one world" was merely a utopia until the breathtaking revolutions in modern science and technology, especially in the field of communications. Of course, *Vasudhaiva Kutumbakam,* "the world as one family," has been there in India since the Upanishadic times. But the history of human civilizations shows that each one developed independently. Contacts between civilizations were now and then established but they were mostly for imperialistic and aggressive purposes. The Hebraic and Hellenic civilizations were overshadowed by the Roman conquest as the Eastern civilizations were distorted by the Western colonization. After millions of years, the various countries of the world have converged to live in the "global village".

Emergence of UNO

The disastrous First World War compelled the world leaders to float a global organization called the League of Nations in 1920 for a safe and secure world. But it became defunct and could not prevent the Second World War. Then was established the United Nations Organization (U.N.O.) in 1945 for a peaceful, harmonious and cooperative world. The various organs of UNO like the International Court of Justice (ICJ), the International Labour Organization (ILO), World Health Organization (WHO), Food and Agricultural Organization (FAC), United Nations Educational, Scientific and Cultural Organization (UNESCO), United Nations Development Programme (UNDP), United Nations Human Rights Commission (UNHCR) and others have been working world-wide to achieve the aims and objectives of UNO.

World Trade Organisation

An offshoot of the United Nations Conference on Trade and Development (UNCTAD), the World Trade Organisation (WTO) has ushered in the era of economic liberalization, market economy, stiff competition, quality products and services and so on. These are the salient features of the current globalization process. Most of the countries of the world have literally been forced to join in this liberal economic venture after the General Agreement on Trade and Tariff (GATT) was supplanted by the WTO. Of course, the International Monetary Fund (IMF) and the International Bank for Reconstruction and Development (IBRD), popularly known as the World Bank, have largely contributed to the successful establishment of the WTO. The main emphasis has been to open up all the markets of the world for free and unrestricted manufacturing and marketing of products and services. Consequently, the protected, nationalized, and subsidized economy is being discouraged steadily, even though the state governments are caught between the Soylla of the World Bank and the Charybdis of their vote banks. The sail is not smooth but is expected to bring about changes for a better world.

Globalization of India

Today no country in the world, including India, can afford to isolate itself from the ongoing rapid process of globalization. Economic liberalization in India is almost a decade old phenomenon. A number of multinational companies have come into the country. Corporatization of huge public sector undertakings has already taken place. Indian Airlines Limited, Indian oil Corporation Limited, Oil and Natural Gas Corporation Limited, Gas Authority of India Limited, and so on are good examples of this process. Disinvestment from many public sector undertakings is on the card. In course of time the university system is likely to be privatized. People have begun to realize that resistance is of no use. Utter disillusionment with the fifty years of Indian Independence seems to be working behind many of the privatizing initiatives.

As the advocates of globalization have pointed out, it is essentially a means of meaningful growth and development. India can catch the markets of other countries as others will have their markets in India. Now goods and services of international standards can be made available to the common people. Most of the unhealthy monopolized trade practices can be checked. The non-productive and non-viable economic sectors will be compelled to arise from their long slumber. The people of all sectors now realize that they have to work to earn their bread and not treat the customers non-challently.

There are also disadvantages of this globalization, especially to the poorer sections of the society whose earning and buying capacity is next to nothing. The small scale industries will have to face the challenges from the multinationals. India, having the second largest population in the world, will have to look after the food, shelter, clothing, health, education, and employment of the illiterate and unskilled people. In Professor Amartya Sen's words, Indian economy has to be people-oriented as against the multinational economy, which is commodity-based. As the well-known industrialist from

Tamilnadu Dr. N. Mahalingam (1998 : 5-6) has emphasized, Gandhian economic principles cannot be sacrificed, if the whole of India has to survive.

Whatever the consequences, India is very much in the thick of globalization. Even some of the sensitive sectors like telecommunications and defence have partially been liberalized. Gradually more such sectors are being thrown open to foreign direct investments.

Educational Implications

Globalization is not an easy rite of passage. It is a difficult and often painful process of coming to the realization that one has to put up the very best for survival. Only the fittest can survive in the toughest and roughest world of competing market forces. As the Director General of the Council of Scientific and Industrial Research and the Secretary of the Department of Scientific and Industrial Research, Dr. R.A. Mashelkar said in his convocation address at the SNDT Women's University, Mumbai : "The meaning of globalization, for a country in stark terms is global competition and in a competitive world one who comes second is not good enough. One has to be at the top to count. The tool that will take a country to a pre-eminent position is knowledge. It gives the country the competitive edge" (Mashelkar 1998 : 15). Clearly then, India cannot be successful in the globalized competitive world, if it does not produce qualitative and profitable knowledge. But knowledge is produced by capable and committed persons only. One Abdul Kalam is not enough for our country. There is a need to produce such great men and women of extraordinary visionary power. At least the "experts" passing out from the educational institutes should be able to understand and achieve the technological vision of Dr. Kalam as outlined in *India 2020.*

There are hundreds of research and university institutions in the country which are exclusively meant for research and development. Engineers, doctors, technologists, architects, information scientists and other professionals are being produced in countless numbers. They are expected to meet not only the scientific manpower requirements of the country but also the knowledge and technology needs. What actually happens in the educational sector is rather unfortunate. The best join the multinationals and/or go abroad. It is the dross that boss over the rest to abuse powers for selfish ends. Of course, exceptions are there but these are a minority and a helpless spectator to the pathetic show of self-destruction.

In an article called "Globalization : Imperatives for Indian Education Sector," Dr. M. Mukhopadhyay, a Senior Fellow at the National Institute of Educational Planning and Administration, has discussed the middle class origins and collusions of globalization and argued that education has a "determining role" in this process. The advantage of India in the globalized context is that its cost of production is less, but the disadvantage is that its quality of production is low. This problem is applicable to all sectors, including education. He adds : "In the absence of minimum acceptable standards both in school, higher and professional education, India loses out on quality of manpower." He laments that the Indian Scientific manpower does not have the necessary "knowledge, skills and scientific attitude" (Mukhopadhyay 1997 : 1). Most experts on education have shared these views in various forums. Then, quality education is the best tool to meet the challenges of globalization.

Politics with English

One of the major reasons for the low quality of higher education in India is absence of adequate attention to the medium of instruction. English was replaced by the regional languages in some universities and was not at all given any importance in many others. At the same time the efforts to produce textbooks and teachers for the changed medium did not give the desired results. However, the change of medium was justified quoting countries like Japan and China but forgetting the different situations in those countries.

What has happened is mindless politics with language. The educational system of West Bengal is a good example. English was a compulsory subject from the primary to tertiary level. After 1977, however, English was withdrawn from the primary level and was introduced from Class VI. At the degree level English was made an additional compulsory language. That meant the students had to appear in the examination but were not required to pass in English. If they got more than twenty marks, it would be added to the grand total. Otherwise, it was immaterial whether they acquired any knowledge of English or not. Further there was also an option for them not to choose English, as they could select Bengali and have nothing to do with English. Moreover, the students who pursued their studies in English could write their answers in their mother tongue. Such unhealthy practices are happening at the postgraduate level too. If Professor Amartya Sen had studied in this kind of educational set-up, could the Indians have been proud of a Nobel Laureate in economics now?

Recently, the people of West Bengal as a whole pressurised the government to re-introduce English from Class I. Similarly, it has also been made a compulsory subject at the degree level. Those students who are capable can make use of English to their advantage now. This kind of lackadaisical attitude to English has affected higher education in general and English language learning — teaching in particular.

Frequent policy changes have their impact on recruitment of teachers, teacher development, material preparation, and even the classroom situations. When the students know that they do not have to pass in English to obtain their degrees, they do not attend classes, buy textbooks, or study English. When the teachers meet with empty classrooms and indifferent students, demoralization is bound to set in. Some of the English teachers may fall in the esteem of the students and develop complex attitudes. To rebuild the conducive educational environment is not an easy task. Once the teachers are used to indifference, they themselves may become indifferent. The new recruits who are ill-equipped cannot do justice to their profession and may harm the students' interests. This is a vicious circle. There is an urgent need to break it and remove the poison at the earliest.

Responsibilities of the English Teachers

Whatever the policies and practices the State and Central Governments may pursue and whatever the circumstances the teachers may be pushed down to, the English teachers have their obligations and responsibilities to the society. The strength of the teachers is that the whole Indian society has an unshakeable faith in English to transform the students into better qualified citizens. Therefore, the English teachers have no cause to worry about their survival. Globalization has added more value to them than before.

It must, however, be remembered that the value is largely utilitarian. If the teachers deliver the goods, that is, enable the students to acquire adequate proficiency in English, they will continue to exercise their magic power. Due respect has to be earned by sincere and dedicated service.

English and Computer Literacy

The peculiar problem in India is that only about three per cent of the total population speak English. This is the major reason for the politicians to oppose English vehemently. However, people are aware to the fact that English is a language of opportunities for good education and employment, mobility to the higher strata of the society, social prestige and so on. It is not uncommon to find poor people sending their children to English medium schools, even though they may be struggling hard for their existence. Their hopes can be fulfilled by the English teachers only. Mere literacy is not enough for them. English literacy is also required. Now computer literacy has become a prerequisite for a successful life. It is in this context of English and Computer technology that the teachers of English have a new and more demanding role to play.

Impact of Information Technology

Globalization and Information technology are two sides of the same coin. If globalization is the end, information technology is the means to achieve that end. Today the whole world can be in one's palm in the form of a palmtop. As a result, the impact of information technology can be felt everywhere — offices, factories, homes, educational institutions, hospitals, railway stations, airports, bus stations, restaurants, giftcorners, grocery shops, and so on. Information technology seems to be the master technology at present. Previously science used to provide the base for technology. Now the role seems to have been reversed, for no science can advance without the necessary technological base. Even fine arts cannot flourish without technological props. A.R. Rahman's heart-throbbing songs speak volumes for the influence of technology on the common man. "The impact of the microprocessor on society may be as great as that of the automobile or electric light" says the President of the Indian Library Association, Mr. P.N. Kaula (1996 : 8). In such a technologically driven world, how can English teaching and learning take place successfully without adapting itself to the changing circumstances?

Computer-Assisted Instruction (CAI)

Teaching aids in education have long been used. The conventional aids like blackboards, chalks, charts, pictures, textbooks, overhead projectors, slides, natural objects, and so on were and still are used by the teachers for the students to teach a particular subject. The Computers, however, are multipurpose mechanisms which can be used by the students themselves without any intermediary. In tune with the paradigm shifts in education from the teacher to the learner, the computers can provide individualized instruction to every student according to his or her ability. Most importantly the students can interact with the computer in different ways — reading, writing, listening, and speaking.

The multimedia computer has revolutionized the learning process to a great extent. It has made available virtual classrooms and virtual teachers. Though human teachers are needed, they are not strictly indispensable. Even very complex subjects can be learnt through the computer languages and programmes like the modified PASCAL, LOGO (Logic Oriented, Graphic Oriented), PILOT (Programming in Logic), and PLATO (Programmed Logic for Automated Teaching Operation), and many others are employed to teach all kinds of subjects, including English. The Internet is widely accessible now. If one knows how to use a personal computer, one can learn everything on the earth. As technological experiments are endless and rapid, more and more advanced systems are coming up frequently for Computer-Assisted Instruction.

Computer-Assisted Language Learning (CALL)

Methods after methods were designed and developed to teach English around the world in the past several years. But none seems to have emerged as the supreme method. Even the latest communicative approaches to language teaching are found to be wanting. In this maze of methods, the Computer method, that is, Computer-assisted language learning (CALL) appears to have an edge over all others. The fact is that the Computers can accommodate the strong features of many approaches. Srivastava (1994 : 11-12) has reported about teaching Hindi to Elementary School children in PLATO. There is a central computer to which any number of terminals are attached. The teacher at the central computer and the students at the terminals can communicate constantly and simultaneously. According to him CALL seems to be very useful for drill and practice and presentation of new items. An experiment with PLATO for language teaching in the USA has suggested for as much as ninety per cent of the learners (Rao 1984 : 448). Computer games also have good potential for language teaching. Rajaraman and Rajaraman (1991 : 257-259) have discussed the usefulness of a game called ANAGRAM for improving the word power of children. CALL can be used for the degree level students, if adequate and challenging softwares are prepared.

CALL in India

It is encouraging to learn from an article of G. Damodar (1997 : 88-97) entitled "Microcomputer-assisted Instruction in English (MIE)" that experiments with CALL have been carried out in a few institutes like Central Institute of English and Foreign Languages (CIEFL), University of Hyderabad, and Regional Engineering College, Warangal. Dr. Damador himself has prepared as many as twentysix modules for learning English through Computer. These modules cover almost all aspects of English, including Letter-Drafting. Some of them may appear to be more useful to the school students. However, they can be used by the college students for remedial purposes or just for checking their proficiency in English. Interestingly, these programmes of Dr. Damodar are specifically tailored to the needs of the Indian students. It is up to the teachers and students to use such programmes wherever the infrastructure facilities are available.

Beginning and Training

To begin with, the CALL programmes can be used freely for the information scientists at the undergraduate level. Next, they can be extended to the science students in general. For these two categories of students, infrastructure may not be a problem. The English teachers of those institutions will have to be trained to use CALL programmes. The teachers should not have any difficulty because computers in general are becoming more and more user friendly.

Teacher training programmes can very well be executed by private institutions like National Institute of Information Technology (NIIT), Ap Tech, First Computers, and so on. Such a step will be necessary for globalization times. Quality and cost effective training can be given to teachers in this way.

Prospects

Perhaps the general arts colleges will have difficulties in providing the infrastructure. In course of time, however, most of the educational institutions are likely to be helped with computers, as the state and central governments have realized the significance of information technology. The Government of Tamilnadu, for instance, has established an apex institution called Tamilnadu Institute of Information Technology (TANITEC) to prepare the people of Tamilnadu for the next millennium. Besides, it has an ambitions plan of achieving total computer literacy in another ten years (Aludiapillai 1998 : 7). Similarly, the government of Andhra Pradesh has collaborated with L & T Infocity to build the Hyderabad Information Technology Engineering Consultancy City, briefly known as Hi Tech. City. Hopefully, the Government will extend the benefits of Information Technology to all educational institutions in the State. The Central Government is late in its efforts to bring the fruits of the wonder technology to the people directly. However, three specific schemes have been announced recently : (a) Vidyarthi Computer Scheme, (b) Shikshak Computer Scheme, and (c) School Computer Scheme. The University Grants Commission and other Central agencies have contributed enormously to the colleges and universities to set up computer centres. The future looks bright and the teachers of English have to ready themselves for the show.

Conclusion

If globalization is an economic process, information technology is a communication process. Both of them have come to affect all aspects of human life throughout the world. Education, including English language learning and teaching, is not an exception. Computers can help improve the standard of English and enable the students of today and professionals of tomorrow to live competitively in the globalized world. The teachers of English can use the programmes developed by the leading institutes like Central Institute of English and Foreign Languages and by experts like G. Damodar. Well-established and self-financing professional institutions may be able to provide the infrastructure. The rest will have to depend on the generosity of the State and Central Governments. Some of the Governments in States like Tamilnadu and Andhra Pradesh have already started taking the necessary steps. The teachers of English will have to realize the new significance the language has gained world over and help their students achieve good command over English through the multimedia computer in tune with the advances in globalization and technology.

Works Cited

Aludiapillai, K. 1998. "Towards an Information Technology (IT) Literate Society." *University News* 36 : 49 (December 7) : 7-8.

Damodar, G. 1997. "Microcomputer Assisted Instruction in English (MIE)," *Kakatiya Journal of English Studies* 17 (Dec. 1997) : 88-97.

Kaula, P.N. 1996. "Information Technology : Legal, Policy and Management Issues." *University News* 34 : 42 (October 14) : 8-11.

Mahalingam, N. 1998. "A Nobel Prize for Development Economics." *Kisan World* 25 : 12 (December) : 5-6.

Mashelkar, R.A. 1998. "The Meaning of Globalization." *University News* 36 : 5 (February 2) : 14-16.

Mukhopadhyay, M. 1997. "Globalization : Imperatives for Indian Education Sector." *University News* 35 : 18 (May 5) : 1-2 & 8.

Rajaraman, Dharma and V. Rajaraman, 1991 (1986). *Computer Primer* rev. ed. New Delhi : Prentice Hall of India.

Rao, Guthikonda V. 1984. *Microprocessors and Microcomputer Systems.* 2nd ed. Delhi : CBS Publishers and Distributors.

Srivastava, R.N. 1994. *Applied Linguistics.* Vol. 4 of *Studies in Language and Linguistics,* Delhi : Kalinga Publications.

5

Information Technology and English Language Teaching

B. Sudipta

The use of computers in English Language teaching in educational institutions is growing but not at desired phase. With recent developments in computer technology, computers have become more user friendly and then enable teachers to utilise them with minimum training. In this paper, various approaches to ELT have been mentioned like ELT Software, access through the internet and two case studies in order to throw some light on the globalization of ELT.

Technology is a more positive approach than the routine academic methods. In future, there will be a wider set of learners who can be offered enriched packages of skill and knowledge. The innovative institutions will enhance their standards in order to gear up for the competition, to build effective "electronic communities" to disseminate, learn and exchange information in the interactive multimedia way.

Nancy Traubitz a teacher in Maryland, had conducted an experiment entitled *A Semester of Action Research : Reinventing My English Teaching Through Technology.*[1] According to her, the tedium of routine academic exercises destroys a teacher and therefore the research was conducted to save her, intellectually and professionally. She reassessed teaching strategies and with her own classes researched the use of technology. Secondly, she formulated questions and began to collect data, simultaneously welcoming a pre-service teacher. She was of the opinion that, anyone born after

1960 knows at birth how to use the computer. In the process of continuing research, even the average students responded positively. The web writing assignments had to be word processed, group presentation demanded hyper text and they also surfed the World Wide Web. Apart from the computers at English departments, they could work on their assignments wherever computers were accessible to them, even at work or leisure. The classroom management issues were time-consuming: for elaborate day-by-day, minute-by-minute, step-by-step instructions had to be written which were duly taped, and slowly traditional classroom decorum melted away. Questions and doubts loomed in the mind of the teacher which were to be dispelled very soon. Till the completion of the initial survey, all the students used the graphic programme in the word processing package to embellish a composition about symbolism and had searched on-line dictionaries to write a composition-length logical definition. They had surfed various sites on the web and more significantly, students who were not academically motivated voiced a determination to complete their technologically-enriched projects. The author believed that problems could be resolved through a process of reinvention of teaching.

I would like to mention another case study conducted by Sonthida Keyuravong of Chiang Mai University, entitled, *The Use of Computers in English Language Teaching in Japan*[2]. The data concerning application of computer technology to ELT were gathered from 14 universities. The report covered three aspects computer facilities, modes of using computers, and language skills and other skills taught through computers.

Computer Facilities

The use of computers in ELT in Japan is increasing at a very rapid rate. The private universities investigated have an average of two to three computer laboratories for classroom use with an average number of 40 machines in one class. In addition, there is at least one self-learning computer room which students can use to work on their assignments. When the laboratories are not engaged with other classes, students can also make use of available facilities in the laboratories.

Modes of Using Computers

In the fourteen universities investigated, computers are used in two modes as follows :

As a Teaching Aid : Computers are used to assist teachers in teaching. They introduce the material which leads to their class discussion and other activities. For example, at Kobe Shoin's Women University, in a reading class, each student reads an article from the computer on a current situation scanned from the morning newspaper or downloaded from the internet. After the students have finished reading, the teacher discusses grammatical structures of the sentences in the article with the students as a class. The understanding of the grammatical structure of the sentences presented in the text will allow the students to understand the meaning of the text. Then the teacher leads a class discussion again, and after that the students answer comprehension questions.

At Kansai University in Osaka, computers are used to assist teachers in teaching listening skills. Excerpts from CNN International News are used to train students in listening and comprehension. The topics in the excerpts are carefully selected to match students' educational background and interests. Students learn vocabulary items from the excerpt in a textbook before being exposed to the news. At the end they answer comprehension questions in the textbook.

As a Teacher : Some universities use computers to teach some aspects of English. In this case, computers do the direct teaching in place of the teacher. In one example, as a requirement, students have to take four English courses and one has to be a self-study course in which they have to use computer courseware to learn by themselves in the computer laboratory. There are, for example, a conversation course, a reading course, and so on. The teachers are available in the class to help them with language problems.

Skills Taught Through Computers

Computers are used to teach various English skills and other skills as well. They are mainly used to teach reading skills such as speed reading, reading comprehension etc. They are also used to assist the teaching of writing skills which include sentence construction, introduction to connectors, paragraph construction and essay writing. In addition, listening skills can also be taught by computers. The lessons are, for example, listening to the news, listening to conversations, pronunciation — others include grammar and vocabulary.

As the internet has become increasingly popular, computers are used to teach informational retrieval skills as well. The skills are useful when students conduct research.

ELT COMPUTER SOFTWARE

Types of Software

Every institution reported using non-CALL software. Most institutions use Word-processing and Spell Correcting software in their ELT writing classes. Other programs included Grammar Correcting software and software in training computer skills, such as keyboard and mouse utility skills. There are also non-CALL software in the form of CD ROMs which included reference materials such as encyclopaedia, dictionaries, thesaurus, and on-line magazines like US Today, CNN, and Time capsule. However, the software is only used as reference material and is not very popular among the users.

Commercial CALL software is also available but not very popular either. Two institutions reported using them to teach conversation, vocabulary, business English, and grammar. When asked why they did not use commercial CALL software they revealed that the software usually does not match the student's needs. Furthermore, copyright concerns are a serious problem since one cannot use a CD ROM with the whole class, and to copy it is illegal. So to use CD ROM for the whole class means buying a site license or buying a CD ROM for every single machine. This can be expensive.

Regarding the production of one's own software, seven out of fourteen institutions reported having developed their own in-house materials, two of which did the job without help from external or professional sources. The in-house software is developed to teach various aspects of the English language, including writing skills at the sentence level, speed reading, vocabulary, pronunciation and grammar.

Besides using e-mail to communicate with other people, students use it to communicate with their teachers as well when they have questions or when they submit their work. Teachers offer help by answering questions posed by students, giving suggestions and commenting on their written assignment. Teachers claim that the use of the internet motivates students to come to English classes and their performance has improved.

Discussion

The use of computers in English language teaching in colleges and universities in Japan is gaining a momentum. However, the development of English teaching software still lags far behind the technology. The software rarely meets the needs of the teachers and the price is prohibitive. Besides, producing in-house software is an arduous and time-consuming job, and on top of that there is the complicated process of obtaining a copyright. Some institutions have reached a solution through joint projects between the institution and a commercial courseware developer to produce ELT software to be used within the institution. The institution provides the content of the aspects of language to be taught to the professional courseware developer of the publisher, who puts the lessons into the computer. In this way, the copyright belongs to both the institution and the company. It can solve the problems of copyright violation and relieve the teachers of the task of developing the courseware.

Another interesting fact is the use of the internet in teaching English language and culture. It has been used as a research and communication tool by English teachers in Japan. Teachers claim that the use of the internet has motivated students to come to English classes and that their students' performance has been impressive. In one university, for example, students use the internet to search for information. They survey the information on the net, search for a topic they are interested in, hold a discussion in an electronic dialogue with the teacher in order to understand the reading texts, bring the text to class for group discussion, and prepare a report to be submitted at the end of the semester.

In the *Modern Language Journal* 81 (1997), there is a book review by Neil J. Anderson, the author being Mark Warschauer of the book entitled *E-Mail for English Teaching : Bringing the Internet and Computer-Learning Networks into the Language Classroom.*

This informative and helpful text contains 7 chapters, delineates from the basics of computer literacy to producing all information in one place of the methods and materials available for implementing E-Mail with second language learning.

The electronic learning institutions will be a source of perpetual knowledge, simultaneously grouping people of the world for a genuine educational experience in cyberspace. Thus the concepts of time and location will undergo revolutionary transition, moreso, because it will be virtually divided into two categories: namely 'physical institutions' and 'virtual institutions.'

Notes and References

1. Nancy Traubitz, *A Semester of Action Research : Reinventing My English Teaching Through Technology* (Maryland : 1998).
2. Sonthida Keyuravong, "The Use of Computers in English Language Teaching in Japan," *Thai TESOL Bulletin,* 10.2 (Aug. 1997).

6

Computers for Teaching English in India: Placing Things in Perspective

D.S. Kesava Rao

1. Introductory

The arrival of the computer has taken the English teacher in India, at the tertiary level, by surprise and has left him breathless — in terms both of the exciting opportunities thrown up and the sometimes uneasy and foreign feeling it generates. The teacher who elects to ignore the computer is compared often with a man driving a bullock cart and the one who uses them with one piloting a supersonic plane. Is this true? To me, this seems a grossly oversimplified version. Our poor country is not yet ready, I believe, to talk of a classroom with a teacher and a bank of computers with learners before them (both computer-literate!). While this is no doubt a happy situation, there are a number of practical difficulties for this to be realised in the undergraduate scene in India. To continue the analogy of the bullock cart, it appears that the sophisticated pilot is still not sure of a "successful" landing, for he often operates in the absence of proper guidance, or, lured by his smart machinery, lands elsewhere. So, I propose, in this paper, to take a hard, critical look at the problem and offer a balance sheet, as it were.

The wonder machine has so far provoked two lines of thinking, each in its own way and extent as biased as the other. The pro-computer school has been carried away by the obvious novelty, seemingly limitless scope and range, not to speak of the ease, of operation. The votaries wax lyrical over the benefits of the interactive instruction now available and the prospect of a mobile text, print accompanied by sound and image. On the other hand, we have the critics who decry the monotonous, mechanical approach, the lack of suitable (that is, suitable to Indian conditions), CALL software and the diminishing value of the human instructor. In fact, recurrent fears have bee voiced over the fate of the resourceful, imaginative and responsive human teacher. Both schools, in my opinion, are off-track. There is an insistent need for placing things in perspective. Perhaps it would be apt and useful to go back in time and review the tools the teacher has had to deal with to solve the dilemma of whether the computer is merely another tool, or....

Odd as it may now seem the first of these tools was the book itself in the remote past — in Plato's time. It was as mysterious and foreign a tool as any of these contemporary machines. The print media was perhaps a handful for those distant teachers used long to oral tradition. Proper use of the new invention, one imagines, might have generated a good deal of confusion, misgivings — and plain admiration. However, the book has survived to become an essential part of our teaching scene. After a long gap of centuries, the audio and video support added to the repertoire. And, in spite of their widespread use, it must be admitted that they have not altogether met the fast-growing changing needs of the language teachers. Many practitioners of the craft are not using them deftly even now. However, the inclusion of the sound and picture has sidetracked many an unwary teacher — and learner — from main business of teaching. And the language laboratory too symbolised another watershed, but, again, while promising much, has delivered little. It is, of course, true that the interaction between teacher-student, and student-student, so relished, had become a reality with the introduction of the booths in the language laboratories. But one might generalize and say that, by and large, the teacher and the machine stand apart, the teaching objectives falling between stools in the process.

The computer, it is claimed, is different. Still, the opportunities that the microchip and the computer — now the internet — provide must be seen strictly as another "new-find", a brilliant toy for the ever-eager professional to explore and experiment with. If one sets out to assess the utility of this small, ubiquitous wondermenace in the framework of pedagogic practice in India, one has to approach the task with circumspection. A fair degree of open-mindedness is an essential prerequisite.

2. Present Scenario

It would be advisable to see how and where the computer fits in among faces is that of defining the role of the computer in relation to the curriculum. For the main cause of concern — though for some liberty — is the very autonomy that the computer brings with it. While the student can interact with the machine and learn on his own, and at his pace, he should be alert enough to see where it leads him. The current CALL programmes need to be carefully supervised. So, most teachers would like to regard the computer as a self-teaching aid at the pre-teaching level. But this is unfashionable and it takes some courage to take a sceptical attitude like this. On the other hand, the immense advantages in stimulating the student and providing access to vast material is to be genuinely appreciated. The learner must be guided in the sequence of the items to be learnt and the machine should not be organizing it for him. The fact is that the CALL software is not in line with the teaching process and is mostly prepared by people with little skills in pedagogy. And, the language teachers are not proficient in the programming skills.

The fact of the matter is best summed up in the words of V.J. Cook, who says the computer is utilising only some of the possible at present. "Typical existing programmes concentrate on a limited area of language and are incompatible with most contemporary teaching models". It is the responsibility of those involved with computers to develop techniques to exploit the unused potential and to make them more profitable to the teacher in the classroom. The teachers too must come forward to approach the new reality with an open mind and learn to cope with it. To quote Cook again, "Without such a bridge, the use of computers in foreign language teaching will turn into a meaningless activity, providing programmes that no one actually wants to use about aspects of language that few people consider important."

3. Computer and the Teaching Models

As it is, the computer is being successfully used in grammar drills, in writing skills involving choice of structures, vocabulary development and, minimally in teaching semantics and oral communication. Again, one may be quick to point out that the computer is handy in teaching reading and writing skills, but of little help in the context of designing speaking and listening activities. The progress here is slow and perhaps not amendable to large classes. And, one must not forget that the strength of the average Indian class is about 80!

This takes us to the issue of the nature and extent of the utility of the machine of the century in terms of its applicability to the various teaching models. Broadly speaking, these models may be classified under four heads.

I. *The Audiolingual Model :* One of the early and, as far as the computers are concerned, influential models is the audiolingual popular in the 60s. This is based on the behaviourist theories of learning with its emphasis on teaching language through stimulus and response, to enable students to use structures automatically and unthinkingly in appropriate situations. The computer lends itself easily to tightly controlled language acquired in drills focusing on grammar or lexis. But the contradiction here is that the audiolingual method highlights speaking and listening.

II. *The cognitive code model :* This is closer to the conventional Indian pedagogy with the stress on rules and conscious attention to the processes of second language acquisition. This mode sets out to give a conscious knowledge of the target language encouraging the learner to develop on his own. Corrections by computer are useful if one approaches the teaching/learning process in this light. But this model too is not very popular with the language teachers now.

III. *The Communicative Model :* This is the most favoured among the teachers — the method in which communication is the goal as well as mode of learning. Communication is taught through communicating in the forms of role-play, games to felicitate exchange of pre-selected information among students or exercises on the discourse structure of texts. Much of the computer work in the West has been done in mother-tongue rather than in the L2 field.

Still the machines play a useful role in encouraging students to put together pieces of information scattered among different groups, the restrictions on the student's language, not withstanding; the computer has an active role to play here in highlighting discourse connectors graphically and providing feedback through multiple choice questions. Present programmes concentrate on the predictability of words as in a close test or on conventional comprehension testing. One may safely say that the combination of computer with this model appears very fruitful and may be developed further.

IV. *The Humanistic Model :* The aim of this model is not to relate the student to the use of language in the external world, but to develop the internal world of his personality and mind. If the goal of the communicative model is extrovert, the humanistic one has an introvert goal. The question in this context, of course, is whether the computer would be able to awaken the sensibilities of the students, develop their cognitive faculties, or encourage their social and emotional growth. In fact, mother tongue and the learner's own culture, rather than L2, have better claims here. Can the computers be made flexible to cater to the needs of different learners? For, the solution has to be unique to each individual student, ELIZA and CHATTERBOX are some of the software available. Puzzles, word games and anagrams are closer to the cognitive mode which figures in the humanistic model.

V. *The Information - Processing Model :* This is applicable mostly in the teaching of reading and writing. Macleod and Lally have produced a handwriting programme for handicapped children. The computer can obviate the need of the learner to produce the letters physically and helps him to move across the page easily. Processing word units is useful in teaching spelling and has been the subject of innumerable children's wordgames — Hangman, Ghosts and so on. Some advanced programmes by Pain (1981) even have a detailed error-analysis scheme. Word recognition skills, eye movements during reading and, at a higher level, vocabulary teaching are all popular applications already. At the next level, the understanding and production of syntactic patterns has lent itself well to computer applications.

The computer is best with the techniques that control the language the most or that treat rules as information to be acquired consciously by the student. But, at the same time, in processing semantic meaning — that is assembling the meaning of the syntax and word units of the sentence into the meaning of the whole sentence — computer techniques are undeveloped and appear to be difficult in future too. Apart from telling the student, following some sub-categorisation rules, that a sentence like, "The book is sleeping" is semantically unlikely, it cannot do much more at present. On the other hand, in teaching language functions, the machine is useful, particularly in handling interactive dialogues (Higgins and Johns, 1984). Yet another rich area is the discourse-processing where the standard techniques of looking for connectives, linking propositions apply. Further, students can do story creation programmes with help from the computer (Press, 1977). But, in analysing pragmatic meaning, that is language as related to the total situation at the moment of speaking — for example, given what I can see around me... given that it is 2 A.M. on a rainy night in July — the computer is of no help. At present, it is possible to teach it only on a small scale, as in JOHN and MARY, where a student can see how a sentence relates to the limited world depicted on the computer screen, but not to our own.

4. The Word-Processor Option

The point of the discussion so far is to show that CALL programmes are not very suitable in Indian situation and one need not associate teaching with only CALL. It is certainly not intended to dismiss the computer as an unsuitable, hi-fi machine. There is another aspect to be considered carefully — that of the computer as the word-processor. In this capacity, it can be extremely useful in the Indian situation. The chief advantage is that control over the pedagogic issues is returned to the teacher. Ken Hyland points out : "Many teachers feel threatened or diminished by the advent of a CALL which appears to act as a high-tech surrogate tutor, directing activities and evaluating student output." Further, the word processor emphasises the process itself enabling the student to go through several versions. It also builds a dynamic interaction with the text. The learner is free from the chilling, patronising response messages too.

There are three major ways in which the word processor can assist the teacher. *Text manipulation:* Here the student changes a teacher-keyed text by modifying, deleting, inserting, re-ordering parts of the text which promote a close study of the text as well as its structure. At the next, more creative phase, it can help text creation through more demanding exercises. These can include sentence and paragraph completion, collaborative writing and so on. Unlike CALL, the word processor accommodates oral interaction. This is possible when the resourceful teacher designs sub-tasks forcing students to discuss across the groups to put together details of a task. Finally, simulation tasks — like producing the front page of a newspaper, or an editorial, or a consultant's duties — can knit teams together. If there is more than one computer available per group, this would even create a good competitive spirit among the learners.

Finally, the perspective to be gained is that using computers in India for teaching English is fraught with pitfalls, and must be tackled with enthusiasm. The atmosphere should be one of optimism, laced with caution and alertness. Too often the teachers tend to adapt to the existing CALL ware instead of adapting it to suit the needs of our curriculum. This is to be guarded against at all costs. Managed properly, the computer can be an invaluable aid to both the learner and the teacher.

7

Online Sources for ELT

S. Thiruvenkataswami

Introduction

Information Technology has brought about a sea change in the area of English Language Teaching. The CALL (Computer Assisted Language Learning) Software, Multimedia packages on ELT, the Word Processing Packages and the Internet have opened up new methodologies and materials for the teaching of the English Language and also opened up new vistas for research and consultancy in the area of ELT and Applied Linguistics. The paper aims at throwing light on some of these.

Internet Facilities

Internet is a network of computers across in the globe. From any one of the computers on this network, one has the option to log in to any of the computers in this network crossing the boundaries of space. This means that one can remote log in to a computer anywhere in the world and operate it from his own work place. For a teacher of English this is useful for obtaining authentic materials from a wide range of genres and subject areas from one's work place and that too in a digitalised form. One can obtain not only texts but also pictures including voice. This is very useful for authors looking for varied materials for preparing their books and even audio-visual materials.

Secondly, Internet facilitates browsing on the world-wide web (WWW). This offers a host of facilities for obtaining texts of varied types from a wide range of countries. This also helps the teachers to browse the sites of other universities in the world, get to know their facilities, research work in progress, names of faculty, their interest, conduct of seminars, conferences, short terms schools at the international level and so on. This is a great advantage to a teacher of English to build an international perspective and also develop wide professional contacts.

Electronic Journal is another offshoot of this new electronic culture. It is possible to get electronic journals in one's areas of interest at the quickest possible time and that too freely. This comes through email. Emails, which have become a common mode of communication today, have been of great help and assistance not only to the English teachers, but also to any one in general. The concept of email has led to another academically rewarding facility called 'Newsgroups' or 'Mail Reflectors'.

Newsgroup is a facility, which brings together like minded individuals and special interest groups (SIG) to share ideas and profit mutually. TESL-L is a very popular 'Newsgroup' facility for practising English Teachers in the world. To subscribe to TESL-L services send an email to listserve@cunyvm.cvny.edu. In your message leave the subject line blank. In the body of the message, write

Sub TESL-L your firstname your lastname

(for example, sub TESL-L Satyaseelan Thiruvenkataswami)

TELS-L services offer several sub branches to cater to the needs of the ESL and EFL teachers who have special interests other than discussing mere general topics through TESL-L services. They are as follows :

TESLCA-L	Computer Assisted Language Learning
TESLEF-L	Fluency First and whole language pedagogy
TESLIE-L	Intensive English Programs, teaching and administration
TESLIT-L	adult education and literacy
TESLJB-L	jobs, employment, and working conditions in TESL 'TEFL
TESLMW-L	material writers
TESP-L	Teachers of English for Specific Purposes.

To join any of these sub-branches one should first become a member of TESL-L and then send an email to the TESL-L LISTSERVE with the message sub xxx-L your firstname yourlastname (where xxx-L represents the name of the list you want to join). For example : Sub TESLJB-L Satyaseelan Thiruvenkataswami

Three letters received from the TESL-L Services are given below as samples. The first letter informs the Thai TESOL ESP SIG 4th annual conference. The second one is a response to one's question about 'Teacher Supervision' and the third is an informative letter about a book on teaching English through pictures. On a daily basis the subscribers to the TESL-L services get such informative letters and also can get reply to their professional queries.

Letter 1

Date sent	:	Sat, 16 Jan. 1999, 08 :50 :31 EST
Send reply to	:	William Martin <williammartin@HOTMAIL.COM>
From	:	William Martin <williammartin@HOTMAIL.COM>
Subject	:	ThaiTESOL ESP Conference
To	:	TESL-L@CUNYUM.CUNY.EDU
X-No-Archive	:	Yes

The ThaiTESOL ESP SIG, in association with the ThaiTESOL Computer SIG announces the 4th Annual Conference : Technology, Methodology & Materials in the Teaching of ESP, March 6-7, 1999, Bangkok.

Details are available from John Morgan, Conference Coordinator

Tel : +66-2-933-1554 ext. 19

Fax : +66-2-933-1602

rdlthai@loxinfo.co.th

http ://www.rdlthai.com/esp_index.html

2303-5 Lad Phrao Rd., Bangkapi, Bangkok 10310 Thailand

Bill Martin <williammmartin@HOTMAIL.COM>
Zayed University, Abu Dhabi

For technical help with TESL-L, write to TESLHELP@CUNYUM.CUNY.EDU

Letter 2

Received : from listserv.cuny.edu (listserv.cuny.edu [128.228.100.10])

by recw.ernet.in (8.9.1/8.9.1) with ESMTP id BAA10802

for <thiru@RECW.ERNET.IN>; Sun, 10 Jan 1999 01:59:46 -0600 (GMT)

Date : Sat, 9 Jan 1999 15:32:12 EST

Reply-To : Theresa Pruetl-Said pruetlst@MARTIN.LUTHER.EDU>

Sender : "TESL-L : Teachers of English as a Second Language List" <TESL-L@CUNYVM.CUNY.EDU>

From : Theresa Pruel-Said <pruetlst@MARTIN.LUTHER.EDU>

Subject : What is teacher supervision

To : TESL-L@CUNYVM.CUNY.EDU

In response to the question about teacher supervision and can teachers do what they want as long as they please the students I would say in the IEP I worked in this was true sort of. Many English Language Programs even those affiliated with universities here in the US are required to produce their own funding which means that if we don't please the students we'll have no program. Research has shown that most students decide upon an English program because someone they know has recommended it so it would be not in our best interest not to please students. However this doesn't mean that chaos reigns. Second we also have to please the university and its faculty so we also have to meet their needs. Since many of our students go on to the affiliated university these needs are not necessarily divergent. But as the previous poster said this also means that we hired experienced professional teachers who had the ability to run their own classrooms, choose their own books, etc. But.... .

Terry Pruett-Said

pruetlst@luther.edu

ESL instructor

NE Iowa CC USA

Letter 3

From	:	JNHajnal@AOL.COM
Subject	:	Teaching Beginners, Drawing Pictures
To	:	TESL-L@CUNYVM.CUNY.EDU
Content-Type	:	text
X-UIDL	:	3c5937e86cdfcd2e248d109f15a0a6df

In addition to the books and dictionaries mentioned so far, Andrew Wright's 1000 PICTURES FOR TEACHERS TO COPY, now published by Longman, is an invaluable source for drawing stick people in various positions (*e.g.* showing movement), faces with different expressions and similar simple pictures quickly and confidently, even if you are convinced that you can't. There is a useful index at the back of the book. (Perhaps this book has already been mentioned — I may have missed it.)

If there is an overhead projector available, it is also possible to trace the picture one wants onto acetate (or photocopy it onto special acetate-for-photocopiers), project it onto a wall, put a piece of paper of the desired size onto the wall, move the photocopier until the picture is the right size, and trace the image onto the paper with a felttip.

The point to remember is that the aim is not to produce an "artistic" product, but to communicate an idea, and students generally understand this perfectly. (If you feel the need, you can add a throwaway comment like "My name is not Rembrandt/Picasso etc.")

If you ever have the chance to attend a workshop given by Andrew Wright, you will be well rewarded!

Nina Hajnal, London, UK
JNHajnal@aol.com

Computer Facilities

Computers in themselves are a valuable tool assisting effective language instruction. CALL Software is a useful aid for classroom instruction and more importantly an excellent resource for self-study. Learners' motivation is rather high to learn interactively with the computer. Moreover computer aided language learning software provides appropriate tasks for students at different levels. These materials are produced by talented experts in the field. The learner can study at his own pace at his convenient time and at a place of his choice. In that sense it has an advantage over the face to face teaching. Some of the available CALL Software items are GAPMASTER, TEXTMASTER, PINPOINT, STORYBOARD, MATCHMAKER, GRAMMAR and VOCAB.

GAPMASTER contains texts where every n^{th} word or the chosen word can be deleted. It is possible to delete all the prepositions or the articles, or the verbs. Students will be able to construct such gap tasks by themselves using this software. When the students work on them they will get to know through the software itself whether they have got the right answer or not. In case the learner goes wrong, the computer will provide certain prompts and enable him to arrive at the answer. Similarly, TEXTMASTER is a software that deals with construction of texts such as arrangement of sentences in the right order, filling in of the correct connecting and linking words, etc. MATCHMAKER is a software that primarily works on certain grammatical aspects or on vocabulary building tasks using the question type 'match the right responses.' STOREYBOARD is software that contains reading comprehension passages.

The software referred to above primarily uses the print medium. But CALL software is available on multimedia also. This incorporates voice too. Therefore, in addition to training learners in reading and writing which was possible in the earlier type of CALL multimedia provided training in listening and speaking tasks too. CALL facilitates not only on-line teaching using computers on a local area network, it also enables evaluation of their performance on-line.

In addition, Local Area Network (LAN) and Wide Area Network (WAN) facilities are very useful for a teacter of English to offer online English Language Training Programmes for students within a college and also for those outside the college. Once he prepares the materials and places them on the LAN learners can access them and answer them at their convenient time. The teacher also can evaluate them and provide appropriate feedback on-line. The author has experience in offering such programs at the REC to a few interested non-teaching staff. It is very easy to provide training in reading and writing throughout such mode. Imparting speaking and listening skills is also possible but it demands an upgraded infrastructure facility.

Concodancers

Another important area where computers have been extraordinarily helpful is corpus linguistics. Concordances are softwares which have the potentiality to analyze a huge chunk of text and order them in certain desirable fashions. For example, it is possible to order a text to pick up all the contexts for the use of the word 'mean' in such a way wherein computer would be able to place 'mean' at the centre and bring forth five words that come to its left and five words to the right. This facility has revolutionised the study of Lexis. It will be possible to study how a word is used by a particular group of people at a given point of time. The modern lexicographers use this facility in compiling their dictionaries. COBUILD is one such dictionary.

Conclusion

Computers have come to our assistance in every walk of life including English Language Teaching. It is another medium for devising ELT materials such as print or the audio-visual mediums. One need not be unduly perturbed by it. Whether one wants it or not there is no escaping from this academically powerful device.

8

IT Revolution: 'Power' Presentation

D. Shobha

I

The turn of the century is heavily marked by the heralding of the era of Information Technology. It is going to be the age when the latest of the technologies is going to be used for creating, transmitting, manipulating, storing and sharing of information. Terms like computer, software, data, downloading, multimedia etc., are going to be the buzz-words heard from all directions.

Over many centuries, the need to communicate and to establish a common mode of communication led to a continuous evolution of several forms of communication. As a result the human race has witnessed the emerging of several oral and written forms of communication as and when the need demanded. Gradually the written form gained a lot of attention and in turn took various forms from carving inscriptions in rock and on tree trunks to writing on palm leaves, to pen and paper to the great inventions of fifteenth century — the printing machine by Gutenberg.

Now for almost five centuries we had been totally pre-occupied with print-medium. People have thoroughly learnt to express and share their ideas and thoughts in printed form. All the information that was generated was printed. As a result enormous storing space and related paraphernalia had to be created. The print medium, thus, continued to reign unquestioned.

II

Today with the advent of Information Technology and computers the entire scenario is transformed completely. This new technology quickly brought in and continues to bring in changes in every aspect of human life. These new changes have ushered in the "Digital Technology" that plays a crucial role in sustaining the new world order. This new Digital Technology is efficient, easy and ever expanding. It shrinks space and time and makes available our world virtually in the form of a globalized village.

At this juncture, it is important for everyone to reflect on and respond to the demands of the hi-tech digital age. Social advancement of all the fields of public interface has to be matched with the development of efficient techniques of communication to sustain the tempo of growth. These new technologies have come to stay and any amount of time spent on discussions to prove whether these are "good" or "bad" will be a mere waste of time. While engaging with the question of how best they can be used for public benefit can be more productive. Education is one area that needs a complete revamping to meet the challenges of IT revolution. Conventional modes and aids of teaching need to be upgraded and new customised methods should be invented for specific purposes.

Computer can be one tool that can help enhance and extend human capabilities. As it is the keystone in the information age, people must have some degree of computer literacy. However, it is not necessary to become a computer scientist in order to use this machine effectively. In other words, an individual can use a computer without being a professional scientist. Several commercial softwares are flooding the market to entice more and more users. Opportunities for careers in the computer-related fields are expanding dramatically.

As training in communicative skills is central aim of English education, we must explore how this training can be imparted in the context of the IT revolution. It seems to me that one of the basic skills such as content presentation can be effectively developed through computer technology. These improved communicative systems can be made more effective with proper presentation skills. As is well-known Digital Technology combines oral, written and aural communicative skills for impressive presentation. Several commercial developing companies have developed tailor-made packages for this purpose.

III

Power Point is one such package made by the software giant, Microsoft. It comes as a part of a larger office automation package called MS Office. This is a presentation programme that can be used to create slides, hand-outs, overhead transparencies and speaker notes. Whether you are making a presentation for a multinational company or for a small business to sell a product, or to demonstrate the outcome of a research project, Power Point is a convenient tool.

This paper is an attempt to demonstrate how presentational skills can be developed using Power Point. The first step in making a presentation is to make a story-board of the topic that goes into presentation. In other words, the key points or the key stages have to be defined first. Care should be taken in writing short and crisp messages or statements. Once the presentation plan and layout is made one is ready to work with the slides in Power Point.

In Power Point we create and edit individual units called slides. In the following paragraphs, for the purpose of demonstration, a description of a model presentation is given. The topic for this model presentation is the theme of the UGC Seminar, "IT Revolution, Globalisation and Teaching of English," where this presentation is made.

In this presentation I have used five slides.

(i) The first slide is used to announce the title of the presentation.

(ii) The second slide introduces the topic of the presentation.

(iii) The third slide explains the theme of the presentational subject (the Seminar).

(iv) The fourth one lists the objectives of the Seminar.

(v) And the last slide provides the scope of the Seminar.

To start the presentation, we have to create a new file first. For doing this click on 'New' in the file menu or the white dog-eared paper icon on standard tool bar or simply press 'Ctrl-n' on the key board. This opens a dialog box, where you click OK. This in turn leads us to the 'Auto Layout' dialog box. This box holds several predefined auto-layout model slides including a blank-slide.

To create the opening slide of our presentation choose the blank slide from the 'Auto Layout' box. This type of slide gives the freedom of using the graphical text, the 'Word Art.' This feature provides an unlimited number of options of scaling, rotating, flipping and coloring of the text. Next, click on the 'Word Art Button' on the drawing tool bar. This opens into "Word Art Gallery" where nearly 30 Word Art styles are available. Choose any one style and click OK. Then a Word Art text editing box appears. Type the first line of the text for the first slide — National Seminar," in our example, and click OK. This text appears on the slide with the pre-defined color-scheme, line size and color and font type and size. Drag the text with the Mouse to the center and scale it as required. Click on the text again and give it the Shadow style 20 through the 'Shadow' button on the drawing tool bar. This gives a mirror image of the text vertically below the original text. Next, click on the Word Art button again and this time choose a vertical style for the text. Type "UGC" in the text editing dialog box and click OK. Move and place this text on left-hand side of the previous text. Scale it until it looks bold and prominent on the slide. To make the slide look more interesting and attractive add clip Art to the slide. Clip Art are the graphics files that are created and loaded into the computer along with the software application.

The next step in creating our first slide is making the logo of the Seminar — a computer on the globe — using Clip Art. To add Clip Art, click on the 'Insert' menu. Next click on the 'Picture' command and then on the 'Clip Art' option. This takes us to the Clip Gallery dialog box. Browse through the images in the gallery images and select the computer image and the globe image and click on 'insert'. Scale the image of the globe to the match that of the globe on the Seminar logo. Next place the image of computer on the globe image and group them. This can be done by clicking on the 'Draw' button and then on the 'Group' option on the drawing tool bar. Place it and the logo is ready just above the title of the slide.

Power Point not only provides a number of text styles and text modification tools; it also has a wide spectrum of background colors and patterns. To give background color or pattern click on 'Fill Color' icon and then on 'More Colors' or 'Fill Effects' option. Select the color or pattern that matches the color of the slide and click OK. There are also several sub-menu options available such as 'Gradient', 'Texture' and 'Picture'. Try matching the colors until an appropriate combination is reached and 'Apply' it to the slide.

The essence of the Power Point lies in the different animation, transition and sound effects we can give to the slide. A Power Point presentation with all its text styles renders itself most ineffective and uninspiring without these transition elements.

A Menu called 'Slide Show' is created specially for this purpose. It provides all the options for slide and text transition. Slide transition is nothing but the changes a slide or text undergoes in its passage from one stage to another. Power Point comes packed with several audio and visual special effects for this purpose.

Our next task is to give these transition effects to the slide that we have created. Click on the 'Slide Transition' option in the 'Slide Show' Menu. In the resulting dialog box, choose the mode of transition such as 'Blinds Vertical' then check the 'Automatically' option and give two seconds as the time for transition. Next choose a suitable sound file for the theme of the slide and finally click on 'Apply'.

Next step is the text transition. Text transition effects can be given through 'Custom Animation' option in 'Slide Show' Menu. From the wide variety of text transition options available choose one and check the 'Automatically' button. (A pre-view window is also provided for a quick view of the transition effects given here.) Every text string and graphic object present on the screen can be given these effects and this brings to an end and creating and embellishing of the slide.

For a final view of the slide click on the 'View Show' option in the 'Slide Show' Menu. The slide that we have created grows to the full screen size and the sound that we have attached to the slide starts playing. All thc transition and animation effects come to life in this view and each slide gives way to the next slide automatically. After going through all the details a final Spell-check can be made. This is necessary to avoid any spelling mistakes in the presentational text on the slides. (This activity can creatively be used in classroom teaching situations.) This Spell-check is done through the 'Tools' Menu. Click the 'Spelling and grammar' option in the Menu and the system starts checking the grammar, punctuation and spelling of the text on the slides. Continue to do this until the computer gives the message "The Spelling Check is complete."

The first slide is ready now. Repeat all the above operations for the remaining four slides to complete the presentation.

IV

What I have presented so far is a demonstration of a new skill that has emerged in the context of new technologies of digital media. This skill can be used as an aid for teaching English. Its audio, visual features make it more appealing in the instructional context. Power Point presentations can also be made interactive with its features like 'Action Buttons' (not discussed in the paper).

It has been estimated that greater and faster learning can be achieved through visual presentations than through listening or aural means. It has been argued that with digital aids like Power Point and Multimedia, the retention capacity of the learner is enhanced. Hence the Power Point, armed with both these features (aural and visual) can be very effective as a teaching aid. The learners can be stimulated and made to understand quickly through presentations made on any particular topic. The topic can be explained through the presentation, which can render it more vivid and easy to understand. This integration of Power Point visual presentation with the oral explanation is very much desired in the rapidly changing scenario of the present.

9

Learning without Teaching: Linguistic Competence of IT Operators *vis-a-vis* their Communicative Abilities

Malathy Krishnan and *Indumathi Ramanathan*

Globalization in a large measure has been achieved in the nineties through the invasion of Information Technology. English as the language of computers has attained a greater degree of world hegemony than in the days of imperialism and colonialism. This has been achieved with absolutely no resistance from the users of the English language worldwide. We are no longer caught in the conflict of interests with the nations that English belongs to. The English language has come to be totally dissociated from the cultural overtones of the native speakers of the language. Millions of computer users in the many Afro-Asian countries are far removed from the spoken variety of English but can cope with highly sophisticated uses of English without ever having encountered native speakers, or without ever being called upon to communicate or interact in English.

This paper examines the restricted use of highly specialised language among IT operators whose level of communicative competence in English is below average. It analyses the language features that these professionals are exposed to and how they learn to perform functions with the instructions and information they receive from the computer itself, that is, the language that a computer uses to talk to its users. It should be noted that this language originates in the United States and is in no way toned down to meet the requirements of non-native speakers of English, the language that the native speakers use to negotiate with on-line.

Computer literacy involves reading instructions and information and acting upon them. It is a level of literacy where the emphasis is on "code as code." Reading is more important than any of the other language skills. The code in a computer is crucial to the performance of the functions that we can achieve through it. It has been observed that computer operators achieve a high level of efficiency in performing functions in the basis of computer instructions, which people with high literary and creative sensibilities in English do fail to comprehend.

These observations have been triggered off by observing IT operators at work in a processing centre. There was a great deal of interaction among the half a dozen operators in the room about how to solve problems while using the computer. They were learners who did not use English for personal interaction. They were all Telugu speakers drawn from a semi-urban background. The interaction was in a bilingual mode. All the technical content words were in English while the other peripheral functional/structural elements were in Telugu. For example "Mac active *chei.*" "*Akkada* track *chesthe Ikkada* mount *aithadha*?" A linguistically complicated piece of instruction like, "access privileges denied, fault in shared networking," was quickly interpreted and communicated saying "sharing disconnect *ayindhi ra.*" There is a great deal of shared information that makes these professional interact with each other in advancing their computer literacy. Most of this literacy is acquired on the job rather than from what they have received from the English instruction received in school or college.

Computer language has a highly specialized code. This involves specialization at two levels : vocabulary and structure. It also involves the use of strategies : looking for information at the right location and the ability to take the help of the utilities available on the software programme.

Vocabulary : The items of vocabulary encountered while using computers to perform functions fall under the category of passive vocabulary. Computer users read and make meaning of words in order to perform functions. But it is very unlikely that they will ever use these words in actual language production either in interpersonal communication or for any other communicative function. Also their understanding of these words will be in their restricted sense in the environment of the computer, and they are generally not interested in knowing their other connotations or even be able to respond to them if used in normal colloquial speech. To go back to our earlier example, the phrase 'access denied' conveys to them that they cannot get into the operative area they wish to in order to perform a function. But they are not likely to use the words in speech in ways that a person who has communicative ability in the language would. For example, they may never utter a sentence like. "The director is not a very accessible person." The phrase is a visual symbol and the two words are understood together in juxtaposition. They may not think of them as individual units and what they mean in a unitary way. They are in the form of lexical phrases that are read as chunks rather than as individual words, as signifiers.

A study of the vocabulary items can be very interesting. Prefixation in a very unconventional way is used to convey various senses. Examples of these are : undo edit, unhide, preview, deselect, despeckle. In fact, advanced users of English might wonder at a word like "despeckle." It can only be understood in the context of picture scanning and reproduction. It is a process by which the fuzzy elements in a picture can be removed to effect a "high-quality resolution." This word, "resolution" again has so many connotations for us except that which is meant in the area of printing. Other examples are : autocorrect, autosummarise, autoformat, autoflow, autoshapes. We will seldom use such prefixes in any other sphere of language use. Interestingly the use of suffixes is quite rare.

Unfamiliar words become familiar through contextualised sense-making. For example, "cached copy" is understood as stored copy although the users may not have known the word 'cache' in its usual sense in everyday spoken language. They thus understand the word in its specialised use more than in its familiar form. They may move from the unfamiliar and the specialised to the familiar and the general sense of the words as used in common parlance. What is being suggested is that the context and the urgency of the function to be performed impose meanings on the words, and they are understood even without a prior knowledge.

Grammatical patterns : Some very frequently used sentence patterns are :

(a) imperatives.

(b) passive constructions, more specifically those with ellipses.

(c) interrogatives : yes/no questions; wh-questions.

(d) nominalisations.

(e) participial constructions.

(a) *Imperatives* : These are the simplest of language structures and perhaps the ones that users with a minimal level of linguistic competence feel comfortable with. But the actual commands can be quite complicated and IT operators learn to understand these commands with more ease than a person with an extensive ability in the language would. This is because they consider the whole instruction as a chunk and know through an ongoing process of experimentation what would actually result in the performance of an action. The command is validated against the success of the performance of the function. A person who analyses the language may get very absorbed in the meaning-making operation to be able to achieve desired results. Thus I have several times failed to open a floppy disk because of reading and interpreting the actual literal import of the message, whereas a date entry operator would advise me to click "no" where meaningfully-speaking I had clicked 'yes'. Computer literacy demands a very different level of reading ability than that demanded by more advanced kinds of reading and interpretation.

There are two kinds of the use of imperatives. One is that used by the computer to direct the user's action. The other is the programmed set of instructions on the means to be selected by the user to give commands to the computer. The first can sometimes be complicated and comes more through use rather than through comprehension. Such instructions sometimes run into several sentences giving options to the users for rectifying procedural errors. The second is simpler than the first consisting mainly of single-words or two-word phrases. Examples : go to, send to, cut, copy, paste etc.

(b) *Passive Constructions* : Computer users get more exposed to passive constructions that report the status of operations being performed than they would encounter or use in everyday language of communication, *i.e.,* in real-life settings. While this is true of most examples of academic or professional discourse, its use in more predominant in computerese. Moreover the passive sentence structures come with ellipses, such as, "items being processed" "items being copied" etc. These are passive forms of the present continuous tense. The IT operators are at a level of language expression where they are more likely to use the active present continuous form for these actions rather than the elliptical passive forms. They are more likely to say, "It is copying" or "it is processing" rather than "being processed" or "being copied." We also encounter uses of the present perfect in elliptical passive forms, such as, "host contacted."

(c) *Yes/no Interrogatives* : These questions demand decision-making by the users. These can often come in structures using the modal verb, "would" as in "Would you like to revert to the previously saved version?" They may also be questions requiring confirmation, such as, "Are you sure you want to send this to the recycle-bin?" There can also be direct Wh-questions in the multiple-choice format, as in, "What do you want the computer to do? Shut down, Restart, Restart in the MS-DOS mode." All that the users have to do is decide upon the course of action and click the appropriate option.

(d) *Nominalisations* : As in most cases of academic and professional discourse, computer language makes a great use of nominations, especially for the listing function. For example :

Opening, Creating and Saving documents.

Typing, Navigating and Selecting.

Editing and Sorting.

Checking Spelling and Grammar.

Formatting.

Importing Graphics and Creating Drawing objects.

In addition to this status reporting, communications by the

computer are conveyed in the elliptical present continuous form as in : verifying data, dialing, contacting, waiting for reply etc.

A more complicated expression can run like this : "Dial-up networking could not negotiate a compatible set of network protocols you specified in the Server Type settings. Check your network configuration in the Control Panel then try the connection again." It is obvious that such status reports and remedial action comes couched in a vocabulary that is highly specialised. Unfamiliar words account for nearly 30% of the total number of words in this sentence in addition to the structural elements.

Reading Skill : We could not turn our attention to the reading strategies that computer users get accustomed to. One very noticeable strategy is the ability to sift essentials from non-essentials. They get experienced in selective receptivity to incoming information. In addition to this several sentences are read together as a chunk. In fact, it would be more appropriate to say that there is little sensible reading involved here. The written matter approximates to a visual; symbol and is decoded without actual deciphering. All this increases their speed of responding to the communication presented by the computer. They attain a high level of reading ability with regard to the language they encounter on the computer. This speed reading ability may not match their actual reading ability of written material outside the computer environment.

It is obvious that there is hardly any instruction that computer users receive in the linguistic features listed here. It is acquired by the users on the job. A high degree of motivation to achieve results helps them in comprehending this highly specialised genre of language. The instruction that they receive, as part of their computer training programme, too does not focus on the linguistic features. Any help that they get is from going to the tutorials, accompanying software programmes or the help/demo menus. These in turn orient them to the kind of language they will encounter in computer use.

The inventory of highly specialist passive vocabulary and structures may not be activated in real-life communication. But perhaps when the need to communicate becomes urgent all this passive absorption of language will help them to overcome communicative barriers, thus proving the adage that "language is what language does."

10

Need for Restructuring Teaching Material in the Context of IT Revolution

M. Prabhavathi Devi

This paper discusses the need for restructuring the traditional teaching materials in the context of IT revolution, and the methods to achieve it.The present era is marked by astonishing developments in science and technology. Computers are one forward step in the continuous drive of the human race to master its environment. We are able to interact with machines for storing and retrieving information not only at home but anywhere in the world with internet facility. The facilities of conveyance and communication have made the world a global village. With the pace of change increasing, almost all countries are becoming heterogeneous, cosmopolitan, and internationally aware, and also are exercising significant roles in world affairs.

Today, computers are playing a significant role, especially, in education. To facilitate computer education, English language learning has become a necessity; as 80% of the information in the world's electronic retrieval system is stored in English, which has progressed to the status of a world language (Crystal, 1987 : 358).

The historical impact of English exercises a continuous influence on multilingual India. India has paved the way for reducing the power of language barrier by promoting English to the status of the Associate Official Language. English is taught as the second language in Indian colleges. Still English is the language of many important newspapers, business, academic conferences, science, technology, medicine, diplomacy, sports and so on. However, the methods and materials used for teaching/learning English in colleges have not improved.

English language learning is not simply a matter of language learning. It involves the acquisition of all the knowledge and skills. It is learnt especially for the purpose of communication. In this respect, fluency and accuracy are two important abilities achieved only by hard work expended over a considerable period of time. It is obvious that some learners are succeeding to achieve these two and some others are not. Some of the factors that govern the success or failure in learning English are as follows :

1. the soundness of teaching methods.
2. the attitude and motivation of the learner.
3. the adequacy of resources.
4. the chance to put the language to active use.

There are various teaching methods and some of them involve all the four language skills — reading, writing, speaking, and listening, and some do not. Each method based on a particular view of language learning, usually recommends the use of a specific set of techniques and materials which may have to be implemented in a fixed sequence.

The method of teaching, for English in India, is the same old teacher-centred one. It has not changed though the world is changing. The teacher is the active participant, and the student, the passive listener.

Usually, the college teachers are invariably faced with the problem of lecturing to a large number of students, and the process is generally a one-way communication. The teachers try to cover the syllabus because of the pressure of the time-table, holidays, examinations, etc. rather than uncover it for the students to explore, analyse and critically study in order to assimilate the knowledge and make it their own.

Among learners, there are important individual differences, especially in personality and motivation that can directly influence the outcome of the teaching. Then learners are responsible for their own failure. Some students are motivated, come regularly, show interest, make notes, and do reference work. Some others occasionally come and lack interest to gain knowledge and skills.

Students adopt different learning styles depending upon their individual differences. The teachers cannot rely totally on the teacher-centred method or a single approach as it is likely to be inadequate.

The teaching materials consist of course books, meant for detailed study and non-detailed study as well, designed on the traditional lines, and include the following :

For general English :

— prose with serious essays and sometimes didactic in nature, and long narrations of events or incidents from the lives of famous people,

— abstract poetry,

— grammar with inadequate information and written by non-linguists (in most cases).

For special English :

— prose, poetry, dramas (usually Shakespeare's with the 16th century language) and novels,

— history of English literature and language (which deals with topics such as origin of speech, Old English and Middle English).

Such materials are chosen more for their prestigious content than for their interest or level of linguistic difficulty. These materials do not help to meet the spoken language needs and interests of today's language students. Learners do not find any chance or opportunity to put the language to use.

Language changes because society changes. Language is devised to express the new facets that society develops. In recent years, with the advent of computers, new areas of expression have emerged. The young are showing enthusiasm for English studies. English is learnt to meet the demands placed upon it as a medium of national and international communication. It gives a strength to learners to meet people from other countries on equal linguistic terms. The learning of English ensures greater access to world opportunities. Success in the international world of commerce and industry is becoming more and more dependent on English language learning. Young people now find that they have more career opportunities when they know English, and are moving to places where some degree of English competence is required of them. It enables them to become secretaries, marketing staff, business executives, etc. It provides a valuable perspective for people. It gives them power. For this reason most of the learners are joining private institutes for learning spoken English.

The time has come for learners to play an active role in education. Today, they wish for a wider range of linguistic experience and feel the need for more creative work in speech production. In this respect, the teaching can be viewed as learner-centred one.

Now, there arises a need for restructuring the teaching materials to facilitate the learners of English in colleges, and to enable them to meet the challenges ahead especially in spoken language situations, in the era, technologically advanced.

A vast variety of inexpensive printed materials can be used for teaching — Course books, workbooks, programmed texts, significant literature, newspapers, magazines, charts, pictures, etc. These may be supplemented by expensive technological aids such as language labs, audio and video tapes, records, slides, projectors, film strips and to top the list, computers, despite their limitations.

The teaching materials may be designed, carefully, keeping in view the following :

- Topics must be interesting, stimulating, motivating and relevant to contemporary life — current affairs. They must reflect the social, religious, economic and political conditions, and also the cultures, customs, habits and languages not only of India but also of other countries in the world.
- Prose may consist of short essays, narratives with different structural patterns — usually from simple to complex levels.
- Dramas must be included to enable learners to use the dialogue form. Even Shakespeare's plays may be presented in a revised form, using the current English.

— Interviews, commentaries, speeches, etc. may be included to develop strategies of conversational interaction.

— Something about the latest developments in science and technology may be incorporated, *e.g.,* computers, not only the theoretical part, but also their operation.

— Clues to pronunciation of a standard variety of English must be given, because English does not have one-to-one correspondence between spelling and pronunciation.

— Topics may be designed as to involve all the four linguistic skills — reading, writing, listening, and speaking, and more emphasis may be assigned to speaking skill.

— Grammar must be designed by expert linguists.

— Interviews, commentaries, speeches, etc. may be included to develop strategies of conversational interaction.

— Topics may be aimed to recreate varying situations involving a wider range of linguistic activities such as requesting, thanking, complaining, and instructing.

— Introduction to the sound system of a standard variety of modern English must be made, instead of topics like Old English and Middle English.

— Programmed texts may be designed to save the time and energy of teachers and students as well, and can be handled well on computers.

— Evaluation of the learners must be based on written as well as oral performance.

Considering the above features, it becomes imperative to say that the existing teaching materials for English must be restructured. Materials must inculcate some sense of involvement and independent creative thinking. They must help learners to overcome insecurity, develop confidence and also meet the demands of social and personal relationships encountered at home and abroad.

11

IT Revolution — Traditional Teaching Materials — Need for Re-orientation

C. Surya Sree

This seminar focuses on an area in which all of us are involved as teachers. Looking back on the teaching of English at College level, in the post independence era, and speculating on the challenges of our profession in the next millenium are not tasks to be taken lightly. I venture to present a modest sketch of our future responsibilities and roles in the context of Information Technology and Globalization.

We are at the threshold of Information Technology revolution which will fundamentally restructure the way we produce, work and perhaps even the way we think. At the heart of this constructive fire, lies the genuius of the fresh entrepreneurship driven by scientific and technological paradigm of a much higher order. The following changes at the national and international level are likely to take place. The first and foremost is a further extension of the already extended human life span. Close on the heels comes the next issue, a blurring of the boundaries between the machines and human beings.

India with its massive person power and deeply embedded scientific, mathematical traditions has the potential to emerge as a global economic power in the next millenium. However, the challenge lies in converting mere labour population into enriched human capital suitable for the dynamics of information age. This will require a massive political consensus and a thorough understanding of the widespread revolutionary benefits of the infotech revolution. Founded on such clarity, Govt. policies will automatically nurture and garner gigantic entrepreneurial energies that lie latent today. The final challenge will be in training, retaining and reculturing our billion people, particularly the young towards the goal.

Of all the social institutions, educational institution should be the first to address these issues and a sound basis for confronting these problems should be developed. No curriculum can overlook the modifications. Thus education for the future should not be a push from the past but be a pull from the future.

However, Education becomes integrated with economy. So a well educated community, with sound basis in vocational skills has to be developed. This is where the need for change in curriculum arises.

Students in our Colleges must develop different kinds of skills. They will need to have a far greater degree of sophistication of knowledge about economy, politics and geography of the regions where they live.

They also need to have qualities of a healthy mind. Their ideas should have a sound basis in reality and at the same time lead to future convictions. Their minds should be open to new ideas and reasoning.

To achieve all these aspects, educational system needs strategies, for integrating the future into every aspect of their work. The details may vary from place to place. So careful thought should be given to curriculum framing, evaluation and quality control.

In fact we do not need new curricular packages or more courses of integrated studies, or need we improve the traditional subject discipline. In short the key lies in educational technology. Teaching methods have to be taken into consideration not just the syllabus or the examination, but one's methodology should aim at fostering a "healthy curiosity." We should remember that education is a fire to ignite the minds of the young, but not matter to stuff their minds with.

At present we are cultivating only learning and the ability to learn. The ability to learn should be developed. If it is cultivated, combined with healthy curiosity students would master anything, even if it is outside the syllabus.

Auto learning should be facilitated through project works. Awareness of the areas of the study and mastery in course of time can be achieved through this. The student will identify his own strengths and weaknesses and solve his own problems.

Concept learning should be promoted. Every lesson has a hidden concept. It should be realised by the students ultimately. The chain of concepts that are mastered in one year will automatically lead to another year. To achieve this end, appropriate questioning techniques have to be adopted.

Individualized instruction methods can be practised in the case of slow learners. The teacher after introducing the topic can allot the portion to be covered and the time available. Student should utilize the available learning aids and materials in self pace. Later through group discussions doubts could be cleared. Thus the advantage of the individual learning and that of group methods are combined. Incidentally the oral and aural skills get promoted.

Reference skill in students and teachers need to be developed. This will aid in keeping touch with research and development. There doesn't end the problem. Values should be imparted. Man without knowledge cannot keep abreast of time but knowledge without character is dangerous. So cultural education should definitely find a place. Practice and appreciation of arts is a must to develop our aesthetic sense. Finally a sense of time and place has to be developed. This is the crux of being disciplined. As modern life is a race against time, alertness and quickness on the part of the students should be taken care of.

Communicative abilities are to be developed. The need of the hour is the strong foundation which enables the students to face the explosion of knowledge and information at the click of the mouse. Learning activity has to be rescheduled to keep in tune with the growing frontier of information technology. The boon in the computer industry and the fast changing economy makes it imperative that there should be newer avenues of learning which ultimately link the entire universe.

12

Critical Pedagogy and Global Networks: Re-turning English Today

D. Venkat Rao

Textual Literacy

Digitaracy, literacy through/in digital media, will displace the dominant conception of literacy prevalent in our epoch. The literacy that is dominant today is entirely dependent on the codex form and technology. Consequently, the mechanisms for dissemination of this literacy have been governed by the codex culture. Print technology and printed paper have been the governing means of production and distribution of literacy until recently.

Despite the revolutionary changes that the codex culture has initiated, it became apparent that the print system not only displaced other prevailing communication systems — associated with gesture and speech — it also imposed a selective process of conversion of extant (scribal) material into the codex (print). In other words, the codex form could contain and reproduce specific (largely "text" only) material.

One of the most serious consequences of this exclusion/inclusion mechanism of the codex culture has been the development of a specific concept of literary as the ability to read and write printed and printable material. The dominant notion of text (moveable type) belongs to the epoch of print culture. Even when literacy of the codex form employs aural and ocular means of perception, their status as communication systems is subordinated to a homogeneous object of knowledge — the printed word. The mode of acquisition of literacy and knowledge are strongly linked to a sequential pursuit of printed symbols.

The prevailing concept of literacy not only imposed sequential and linear procedures of learning; it effectively organized various communicational systems in a sequential order. Thus the oral system precedes the scribal which is in turn replaced by the print and audio-visual systems in succession. This chronology is also reckoned as an advancement of learning and knowledge.

Digitaracy

The distinct feature of digital technology is its non-sequential display of various communication systems such as aural, visual and scribal-textual in a singular virtual space. The simultaneity of access to these systems, made possible by the new technologies will displace the dominance of the "textual". Access to information systems is no longer confined to or controlled entirely by the codex literacy (this does not necessarily mean that the "pre-literates" will master PC programming). If the world's communicational and visual archives can be maintained on that non-sequential, non-phenomenal space they can also be accessed through non-linear aural, oral and ocular means. Today the cyberspace makes such access to world's diverse resources possible.

Yet, although already enormous, the resources of cyberspace are at their emergent state (the Net is said to contain some 700 million pages — whereas the Library Congress is said to possess some staggering 100 million-book collection). Moreover, they are largely about Western material. A new literacy is essential not only to access the newer archives but even to contribute to or compose alternative archives, or even to draw newer connections among available archives and communication systems.

Located on the verge of a new communicational breakthrough, it is imperative to reflect on and gather together our skills and resources to meet the challenges of digital literacy collectively. If the codex form of literacy governed our literacy and determined our pedagogical and material output for decades, now it is time to forge new pedagogical strategies and novel materials for use.

Given that the newer technological apparatuses are encroaching upon us in unimaginable ways, what are the ways open to us to negotiate with the effects of these encroachments? What should teaching be that, from the receiving ends, can face the challenges of new technology that are making and unmaking our world, in newer ways?

The English teacher has a double role to play in the scenario we are sketching here : pragmatic and critical. As English is *the* dominant language of the globe in general and of the IT sector in particular, it opens up new challenges for and demands on not only those who love but even those who dislike the language. Like the dollar bill, it has become the universal medium of conversion. The boom of Indian IT industry is largely dependent on the significantly developed English educational and communicational apparatuses of the country. Let me also, in the same breath assure you that, the codes of world domination are written in English language.

Critical Returns

In this utterly contradictory scenario of crisis and opportunity our pragmatic concerns must be of imparting a new literacy. As the new literacy must also be of a critical nature it should displace the age-old and rather dubious division between materials and methods, between skills and substances. Quite often the great divide between skills and substances manifests as ill-conceived or irrelevant contents for ill-thought formalist divisions of language. As every one knows, learning to use of float in a language can never be equated or measured with memorizing of mechanisms of formation and function of that language. Use of a language requires access or exposure to varieties and subtler uses of that language. Today digital technology provides a possibility of such an exposure. The teacher of English with the mere LSRW skills is ill-equipped to meet the challenges of the new technology.

In conceiving a critical pedagogy, therefore, the basic skills of reading and writing must be rethought in terms of word-processing and hypermedia browsing activities. It is only through these newer sills that we can either tap or contribute to the educational and critical resources of that archive of archives called the Internet.

Faced with a mega archive such as the Internet, how does one find one's way? This is precisely where the critical task of the teacher of English begins. Given that the digital apparatus does not prefer any particular route how does he help the student (and oneself) to search for a path? Here a variety of tasks can be identified for context-specific purposes. The real challenge one will have to face is — how many contexts can one traverse to keep alive our pragmatic and critical tasks? Critical pedagogy must be conceived in such a way that while responding to specific contexts, it recognizes the necessity of moving across contexts, of moving beyond identified contexts. Thus, for instance, the *Wall Street Journal's* recent article (in February 1998) on cotton farmers' suicides could be a significant material for a group discussion in Arts and Science College (Warangal). This, in turn could lead to further exploration into other responses to the phenomenon — which could be used in turn to build newer activities. In short fetishizing of a method or material will work no more. One must learn to receive whatever is available for newer uses and in newer ways.

The entire activity outlined here requires the cultivation of communicational and presentational skills. Digital technology's potential in this area appears to be almost inexhaustible. English curriculum must make presentational packages such as Power Point, editorial packages such as PageMaker, word processing, PhotoShop and Director mandatory. New skills must be imparted along with inculcation of new interests and concerns. I find that one of the most crucial drawbacks of conventional English language pedagogy stems from its total blindness to the question of interests. It developed a schizophrenic divide between skills and interests. Hence the impoverished and irrelevant nature of the wealthy English language pedagogy. The possibilities for exploring new interests in the epoch of digital media are limitless.

Hypermedia learning will allow us to access and think about not only Shakespeare but even about Silicon chip making, women's issues and neural nets, biopiracy and big dams, country-side killings and cholera deaths, flyovers and debt-traps. Critical pedagogy must insist that reception of material; learning/imparting of skills and cultivation of interests cannot be separated easily. The persistent question of such a pedagogy will be : What do you do with what you have?

Global Tangles

In talking about the new literacy of critical pedagogy I do not wish to give you the impression that I am some kind of hitech-lackey boasting of some ostrich-optimism, that I am hopelessly out of touch with the local realities of our "impoverished" country. As I have said in the context of English, even if you dislike IT (English, IT), you cannot escape the consequences of it. Today highly paid bureaucrats and irresponsible media pundits talk about globalization and IT in fatalistic terms : you can't stop it, they proclaim. My stakes in this context are modest :

Given the inevitability of more funds becoming available for the development of telephone/telecommunications sector and the fiber-optic technology that for conventional territorially centred and regulated libraries (whether public or private), the educational sector must, in a forward-looking manner, function from the front lines to tap the unprecedented potential of the new technologies for more radical and heterogeneous purposes. For today, as it is through these technologies alone that the access to world's resources is becoming possible, the spirit and force of this conviction need support and wider dissemination.

It is true that commercial, corporate and multinational agencies have already made a beeline into this arena. As is well known the central orientation of all such agencies is market domination. No wonder, the multimedia titles produced even from within India are exorbitant in price. Further, the commercial-corporate agencies are not really touched by the question of social accountability. It is precisely in this kind of situation that institutions that are backed by tax payer's remittances are required to play a role. At present the 6,000 and odd commercially-oriented non-formal computer training centres and software agencies operating in the country quote exorbitant invoices for their services and products. Given the fact that increasingly it is the service and training "industry" which is going to generate new employment in the country, it must be deemed essential to support public institutions such as universities and colleges for training and imparting service-oriented skills. For, it is possible to operate from these locations and generate newer skills and material. More importantly, when these institutions can operate with a sense of responsibility and are committed to the principle of accountability, public institutions can justify their relevance and show alternative to the devouring spirit of market economy.

For it is the market economy, lovingly labeled as globalization that devours the riches of nations and undermines their sovereignty today. Ironically, it is this very economy manifesting in the form of IT that has begun to devastate universities in the US. Most universities are forced to capitulate to the pressures of corporate IT sector and, in the process, give up their academic freedom. If this is the case of the developed academy in the developed West how will our own fragile educational institutions fare in these global networks? How do we refigure our activity of teaching today? What is to be taught in this digiterate globe? What skills and interests will the teacher of English cultivate? What conflicts will s/he focus on? And for what ends? Shall we look forward?

13

Challenges in English Language Teaching in the Twenty first Century

E. Nageswara Rao

English Language Teaching methodology has been changing almost every twenty years. These changes are based on a variety of factors such as the aims of the learners, the prevailing psychological theories of learning, the linguistic theories current, and the advances and innovations in technology. The Grammar-Translation Method, the Direct Method, the Bilingual Method, the Graded Method, the Language Control Method, the Linguistic Method and Communicative Language Teaching are some of the methods that have been widely used in the twentieth century in different parts of the world. Each method is developed to meet the new demands of and emerging challenges from learners. Every method attempts to absorb the prevailing beliefs regarding the learning process and the nature of language. Also, new developments in technology are quickly utilized in the service of language instruction to make it more interesting and efficient. For instance, we may recall the use of phonograph records, radio, film strips, tape recorders, language laboratories, audio and video cassettes and television for enriching the learning experience of students. The use of one or more of these gadgets by particular individuals or institutions depended on their affluence and their adaptability to technological changes. The methods listed above are all useful and valid. They are reasonably successful in achieving their specific goals.

The situation in ELT is changing once again, perhaps more rapidly than ever before. There is an increasing demand for learning English owing to political changes, economic opportunities, social demands, professional needs, and, more importantly, the Information Technology Revolution which is sweeping the world with the force of a hurricane. In the circumstances, academic life and English Language Teaching methodology cannot remain unaffected.

One paradoxical fact is that against 350 million native speakers of English, there are 1500 million users of English today. Perhaps no other language is spoken and/or used by such a large number of people. Both the native speakers and users of English are spread all over the world making English a global language in a very real sense. There are certain areas such as civil aviation where English is the only language used throughout the world.

The aims of teaching and of learning English language have been changing fast. The emphasis is shifting from a study of English literature to the acquisition of language skills. Utilitarian considerations prevail over cultural factors demanding acquisition or improvement of communication skills which include a whole range of oral and written subskills. Universities and colleges continue to teach largely literature-oriented courses and the syllabi are repetitive and far from relevant to the changing situation. The expanding opportunities for teaching English are quickly seized by private institutes which often do not have qualified and trained faculty, and adequate infrastructure and equipment.

There is a great demand for need-based courses which are also called English for Specific (or Special) Purposes (ESP). The current revolution in Information Technology is both a challenge and an opportunity for ELT. It has been mankind's recurring experience that the more efficient systems prevail over the less efficient ones. So it will be with the adaptation of Information Technology to English Language Teaching methodology.

R.L. Chartrand and J.W. Morentz define Information Technology in the following terms : "Information Technology means collection, storage, processing, dissemination, and use of information. It is not confined to hardware and software, but acknowledges the importance of man and the goals he sets for this technology, the values he employed in making these choices, the assessment criteria used to decide whether he is controlling the technology and is being enriched by it"(121).

The use of the computer in language instruction is no longer a passing fad, but an irresistible trend. Micro-computers have accelerated the pace of change in ELT methodology by providing interactive and individualized learning. They can be linked to other media; they can be utilized for a variety of software such as audio devices, touch screens, etc. The Computer Assisted (or Aided) Language Learning (CALL) is transforming the concept of the classroom, the ELT methodology, the role of the teacher and several related matters. For instance, it is no longer necessary for the students to meet in a traditional classroom at a specified time and listen to a teacher. The students may be scattered over a large area and sit in front of their computers and press a few keys to learn their lessons. Computers facilitate distance education by providing it to large numbers of students, and at times and places convenient to them. Computer networks also provide communication among students without the teacher's intervention.

The students using computers can work or learn at their own pace. A course through computers makes the student more actively involved in the learning process. He will have more fun learning and learning through his own efforts. As Martin Phillips observes: "The computer offers a tool to students which allows them to assume mastery of their own learning experience."

The impact of the computers on teaching materials is also significant. Instead of being fixed, they can be modified to suit the needs of individual students. The teaching methodology has been revolutionized with the introduction of computers. For instance, the visual impact of graphics used in CALL can be purposeful and interesting.

Computer cannot replace the teacher, but he will have a rather different role than the one he has been playing hitherto. He may programme the materials and supplement them whenever necessary. It is the teacher, not the technology, who should have the power to make decisions. The areas of human and mechanical action and the roles of man and machine in the growing educational enterprise should be clearly demarcated. With the introduction of the computer as a powerful teaching device, a new balance between the computer, the teaching materials and the teacher has to be struck.

The advantages of CALL are many. It promotes interactive learning because the learner transmits a message and receives one in return. It involves the students personally and emotionally to a greater degree than a printed text can. It provides immediate feedback; the mistakes in learning are notified immediately. The mistakes are pointed out and explained. The learner is guided towards the correct answer. Congratulation messages for right answers flash on the screen to encourage the student. Another advantage of CALL is individualized instruction which is sometimes known as flexistudy (Flexible study). In this type of learning, each student learns at his own pace; slow learners need not feel they are rushed and fast learners need not feel bored with the slow pace of activity. The learner can choose from a variety of programmes to suit his ability and interests. CALL is learner-centred unlike several traditional modes of learning and teaching. It takes into account the learner's strengths, weaknesses and problems and it is geared to the learner's specific needs. Yet another great advantage of CALL is its outreach. It can be used and used effectively even in such places as hospitals, prisons and offices which are generally considered not conducive to learning.

Word Processor which is a product of Information Technology is a useful tool for teaching/writing. It helps in different stages of writing such as pre-writing, writing, revising and editing. The computer can have multiple functions : it can be a tutor, a partner in language games, a guide, a reference book, and a generator of examples.

Language teachers have been making use of the developments in technology. They realize the power of teaching language through various media to explain meanings, to reinforce memory, and to reduce boredom. CALL combines in itself both audio and visual materials and it excites the curiosity of the learners much more than other devices used till now in language teaching.

Francis Bacon who was hailed as the wisest and brightest of mankind by Alexander Pope, said nearly four hundred years ago, in his "Of Heresies" : "Knowledge itself is power." In his *Novum*

Organum I, he elaborated this dictum : "Knowledge and human power are synonymous since the ignorance of the cause frustrates the effect." We need to modify Bacon's aphorism to suit the modern context to : "Information itself is power." The visionary poet, William Blake, wrote more than a century ago in his "Auguries of Innocence" :

To see a World in a Grain of Sand
And Heaven in a Wild Flower
Hold Infinity in the Palm of your hand
And Eternity in an hour.

The 'Grain of Sand' which can reveal a whole new world seems to be the silicon chip.

Note

The three terms, *information*, *knowledge* and *wisdom*, are defined in *Webster's New World Dictionary of the American Language* (College Edition) (1960) in the following way : *Information* applies to facts that are gathered in any way, as by reading, observation, hearsay, etc., and does not necessarily connote validity. *Knowledge* applies to anybody of facts gathered by study, observation, etc., and to the ideas inferred from these facts, and connotes an understanding of what is known. *Wisdom* implies superior judgment and understanding based on broad knowledge.

Works Cited

Chartrand, R.L. and J.W. Morentz (1979). *I.T. and Serving Society*. London : Pergamon.

Phillips, Martin (1986). "CALL in its Educational Context." Leech, Geoffrey and Christopher N. Candlin (eds.) 1986. *Computers in English Language Teaching and Research*. London : Longman.

14

English through the Electronic Media

Sudhanshu Ranjan

The English Ambassador in the court of Aurangazeb had to wait for one year for getting any information or instruction from the queen. The letter, he posted, reached London in six months and the Queen's reply came in six months. It took queen Isabella of Spain seven months to know that Columbus had discovered America. That was the world when inhabitants of one region hardly knew people of another region at a distance of a few miles. In 1860s when the first telegraphic lines in the U.S. were being laid between Texas and Maine the Internationally acclaimed litterateur, H.D. Thoreau, exclaimed : "What people of Texas would have to say to people of Maine?" In the next one century the science and technology moved forward with such a breakneck speed that Marshal Mcluhan had to coin the term "global village" to suggest how the world had shrunk. The shrinking process is still on with major imbalances tilting the flow of information.

Obviously electronic media, especially T.V., played the most prominent role in the shrinking of the world and finally we have come to such a pass when globalization has become a buzz word. Liberalization of economy has further reinforced this process. Perhaps the civilization has moved a full circle. What our forefathers did thousands of years ago without comfort provided by the startling innovations of science we are doing it now with the support of science. Hieun Tsang, Fahien, Ibn Batuta and several inquisitive and daring travellers traversed the globe in order to slake their curiosity about the world. No passports or visa were required. But then with the growth of civilization restrictions were imposed on the free movement of man. Again we are moving in the direction of lifting those restrictions. Now world-wide interdependence and globalization are major forces in contemporary life. Even the international commission on education for the Twentyfirst Century in its report to UNESCO has underlined "... the growing tendency, in the political and economic spheres, to resort to international action as a way of finding satisfactory solutions to problems that have global dimension."

In this age of globalization need for a global language is being felt deeply. Obviously English is the one language which occurs to every one's mind for doing the needful. Electronic media, particularly television, is playing a twin role in regard to language — it is popularizing a language and also destroying it by contaminating its purity.

Language is an essential ingredient of culture and if the purity of language is adulterated so is culture. "Man imitates before he discriminates" is a well-established principle of psychology and television accentuates the tendency to imitate. In the context of India both Hindi and English have been affected, rather bruised, by this tendency giving fillip to mixing of code on a wide scale. Hindi has been anglicized and English has become Hinglish. This mixing of code has given rise not only to unisex language where even girls frequently use words like 'sala', 'yaar', etc., but it has made conversation in one language extremely difficult. Even Hindi words are being used in an anglicized form in English like 'taloing' etc. TV is bequeathing legitimacy and credibility to such a language.

As linguists know that borrowings in any language are inspired because of either need or prestige. Common people imitate the language of ruler and the elites. That is why this tendency to imitate is very pronounced among cockney elites who feel elevated by using the words and language of the elites. This is not always done consciously but more often than not such words creep into the vocabulary of the people and their colloquial languages surreptitiously without any overt effort. Sometimes we find even an illiterate person using all the English words except verb as a coolie saying "express train late hai." Many TV channels even preferred such a languages in the name of colloquialism *e.g.*, Zee TV's News Bulletins. But this channel had to water down and rather revise its policy in the face of carping criticism. Some English words are frequently used in Hindi News Bulletins as if they were more telling and communicative, *e.g.*. exclusive interview. English was the language of our rulers. History is replete with examples which conclusively prove that every subject wants to learn the language of its masters.

The borrowings are at all the levels — syntactic, lexical and semantic. At the level of semantics we find that some words have acquired new meanings (*e.g.*. media) and some new words of information technology have got international currency, *e.g.* internetting, uplink, downlink, teleconferencing, phone-in, etc. Mixing has a special meaning in T.V. All these words are conveniently used in Hindi and other Indian languages. There are now several dictionaries of information technology.

Since the literate class in India understands English, it is more vulnerable to the invasion of English culture which has made inroads in the form of Coca-Cola, Micky Mouse, Spider man, Superman, etc. 'Fast food' and 'hot dog' are not only commonly used in India, these have become popular food items also. Children have become very gullible to the American expressions as they are visually quite sensuous. It influences even their gestures and body language.

All these are symptomatic of cultural atrophy which is symbolized by change in gesture, dress and food habits. Its trickle-down effect is perceptible on the lower classes also. In fact this literate class is not able to discriminate between westernization and modernization and the television has further blurred the line of demarcation between the two. Cut off from their cultural moorings people fail in paying proper respect to their elders. They will call their elders by first name which was never part of the Indian culture.

Humility is intermingled with the Indian culture. Language and culture are inextricable intertwined. In the Moghul days there were numerous ways of addressing the King — Zille-Subhani, etc. In Arab there are innumerable equivalents for the word "Camel" as camel is part of Arab culture.

Macaulay made no secret of his motive when he wrote, "we should form a class of persons, Indian in blood and colour but English in opinions, in morals and in intellect". His strategy, rather stratagem, paid off.

The history of systematic instructions in English literature at Universities in Britain and the USA is not old but dates from the second half of the nineteenth century. The first professorship of English was instituted at Glasgow in 1862. But India does not lag behind much in English teaching. In fact, Lord Bentick invited Macaulay as far back as in 1834 to preside over the General Committee of Public Instruction. This provided an opportunity for Macaulay for writing his famous Minute (1835) and recommending that the spread of western learning could only be possible through the medium of English Language.

In 1854 Wood's Despatch, which is considered the Magna Carta of English Education in India, supported Macaulay's contention. Whether television has reinforced the original design and the supremacy of the English knowing class is still questionable. But despite its reach and impact television has acted more as a corrupter of language than its propagator. Even in Hindi the impact of Punjabi is too glaring to be glossed over.

Though the impact of the visuals is tremendous it also restricts our imagination. The language of television is strictly informative and communicative leaving little scope to play with words. Even in the newspapers the language is crisp and compendious but there is some scope for magniloquence which is strictly prohibited in television as there is no facility to look back and cogitate. This has affected the pursuit for serious scholarship. Children have picked up at the verbal level but there is a marked deterioration in writing with grammatical and spelling mistakes abounding.

A positive aspect of the television is that it has not only brought the peoples of different countries closer but it has a humanizing effect too. People have become more tolerant at the level of language because seeing is believing. Now people of one country can identify themselves with the people of other countries on an emotional plane. Earlier a kind of xenophobia was quite palpable but now a kind of sympathy and even empathy with the people of hostile countries also is discernible. With the help of English this effect gets enhanced especially in the context of India. Sometimes because of distance one does not get involved with problems of other countries but the visual media touches one's sensibility.

The impact of the visual language is perceptible even at sub-verbal level as such values are imbued which are essentially human. Now people are much more aware of the problems of child labour, human rights, atrocities on women, environmental degradation, etc.

At the end I would like to give two cheers to English, not three, as it has not only integrating effect but distancing effect also. It is true that New York and New Delhi are coming closer but is it true of Warangal and West Singhbhum too? Inhabitants of one district do not learn the language of the neighbouring district. The role of Hindi and other Indian languages cannot be overlooked. Child responds maximum to the mother language as he gets acclimatized to that kind of signal right from the womb. After India got independence several universities in many countries opened departments of Hindi because they thought that their diplomatic as well as commercial correspondence would be done in Hindi. As it did not happen slowly those departments were closed.

A kind of conspiracy by the English knowing elites relegated the Indian languages into insignificance. In AIR the news pool was available in English only and the policy decision rests with English Editors. When Tenzing Norge and Edmund Hillary conquered Mount Everest the news was embargoed in AIR till 9.00 p.m. on that day so that it could be first broadcast in the English News Bulletin but the wily Hindi news caster in league with Editor overcarried the bulletin for a few seconds after 9.00 p.m. and broke the news. So though English has a major role on international level importance of other languages should not be underestimated.

This is an age of 'electronic man' as suggested by Mcluhan where electronic media has left print media far behind. With all the shortcomings and negative influences television is the medium of the present age. Print media has dominated the world culture for a long time and so it is not able to digest the advent of a new medium which challenges its very survival. The bias against television is so pronounced that even its strengths have been categorized as its weaknesses. Everyone agrees that its strength lies in its access to even the illiterates. But Neil Postman in his famous book *Disappearance of Childhood* opines that TV has exterminated that childhood because children now watch and understand those things without the ability to read and write for which they would have waited for several years.

Finally, I would conclude that even if TV is bad it is a necessary evil. So we have to think out how best to make its constructive use.

15

Intertextuality

Tecle Ghebremuse

I am concerned in this paper with the problems confronted by students in providing the intertextual links when they are involved in writing their own texts which emerge out of several texts and various other sources. For instance, on the one hand, their compositions are influenced by different texts they read and on the other hand, the mass media, namely, the T.V. and the radio also influence their thinking considerably. Intertextuality refers to all these sources and the inter-relatedness and inter-dependence among texts. It plays a vital role in developing critical reading and in synthesizing texts from sources. It also helps readers and writers create relationships among their prior knowledge and the new knowldge they strive to acquire. Intertextuality also facititates reactivation and search of what has been read and written. It helps readers and writers to find evidence to support their views or to refute others' views. Many investigators such as Hayes and Tieney (1982), Short (1992), Bloome and Egan-Robertson (1993), Hartman (1994) and others applied it to the teaching learning process. School children tell their teachers that some of what they write are the reflections of what they read in newspapers, books, and what they watched in TVs and what they listened on the radios. This shows that intertextuality plays a significant role in the acquisition of knowledge.

Beaugrande (1980) considers intertextuality as the process of interpreting a text by referring to previous texts. Roudiez (1980), who translated *Desire in Language* by J. Kristeva (1980) states, "This (intertextuality — 'intertextualite') French word was originally introduced by Kristeva and met immediate success" (15). Kristeva (1980) also recognizes intertextuality as the "permutation of texts" (36). This reflects the different arrangements, reorganizations and interconnections among texts to make a new text.

Intertextaulity may be considered an indispensable sub-area of academic writing using multiple texts or passages as sources. It has a determinant role in the teaching/learning process. The various interconnections made among different types of texts and with the prior knowledge are fundamental factors in facilitating writing using multiple sources.

Intertextuality is useful to my study because my investigation involves understanding or interpretation (of sources) texts, organization of new texts, selection, connection, generation and integration of ideas, paraphrasing and integration of citations and documenting sources with which intertextuality concerns in one form or another. In relation to this, Bloome and Egan-Robertson (1993) state "intertextuality can occur at many levels (e.g. words, the organizational structure of texts, register levels, genre type, content and the situational contexts in which texts occur) and in many ways (e.g. mixing registers, genres, content and social situations)" (306). Intertextuality is a broad area of study and it makes different meaning to different people.

Researchers in different fields of study approach intertextuality in reference to the nature, purpose and ultimate goal of their investigation and their views of intertextuality. Most researchers/ writers recognize intertextuality as intersection and interpenetration of texts as a whole. As to how it emerged and developed, Wang (1992) states, "it [intertextuality] is an ideological instrument designed to attack the concept of the founding subject as the originating sources of fixed meaning in the text" (7). It has developed to shift the focus from the assumption that meaning is in the text to the view that meaning is the outcome of the interaction between the text and the reader who brings his knowledge of other texts. Wang's (1992) view seems to correspond to the view in theology, for instance, Neusner (1987) referring to the ways the Gospels of Matthew, Mark and Luke share sayings drawn from a prior source, states, "Intertextuality takes place when two or more documents go over the same material and the connection at hand derives from that intersection" (31). According to Neusner's discussion, meaning is fixed in the source text and the reader is expected to discover the meaning and to investigate how the same sayings, for example, interact, intersect and interpenetrate each other. This view differs from Kristeva's (1980) view of intertextuality. Referring to one novel — *Antoine de La Sales* text — she states, "Latin as well as other books (already read) penetrate the novel's text either as directly copied (citation) or as mnesic traces (memories). They are carried intact from their space into the space of the novel being written'' (54). In this case, her discussion focuses on how a text is shaped by other texts outside itself. These outside texts contribute to its production and give it a new life. They invest ideas for future intertextuality. Kristeva does not, however, clearly indicate the types of relations within a single text and she does not also set any criteria to identify intersection of texts as mnesic traces (memories). Regarding this issue, Neusner (1987) says, "Where we have difficulty is demonstrating...intertextuality in texts in which there is no clear paraphrase, citation or commentary" (152). It is important to set some sort of criteria which can help us to identify different segments of a given text. For example, Fillmore (1985) recognizes intratextual, intertextual and extratextual relations as dimensions in language users' knowledge organization. According to Fillmore, intratextuality has to do "with relations between given pieces of a single text" (11). In this case, references, repetitions, and substitutions can help us to recognize intratextuality. The difficulty arises when he refers to intertextuality as "relations between the piece of text at hand and other potential texts or text segments that are partly like it and partly unlike it" (11). Here, he does not clearly indicate how one can identify in what sense potential texts are like the text at hand or unlike it. 'Potential texts' is too general and too vague to convey clear meaning. There is similar difficulty with extratextuality which he refers to as "the connection between a text and its worlds" (11). Fillmore (1985) does not make clear distinction between intertextual relations and extratextual relations.

Bakhtin (1986) notes "the influence of extratextual reality in the shaping of the writer's artistic vision and artistic thought" (163). He points out that sources of extratextual influences are stored in words and he says "these words are the words of other people" (163).

He seems to be mainly interested in demonstrating how texts are continually shaped and reshaped by outside texts.

Hartman (1994) considers intratextual, intertextual and extratextual relations as aspects of intertextuality. He shows how students could produce texts mainly from three texts (through interview). According to Hartman, some students exhibited features of intratextual relations (when they mark their think aloud protocols of the passages, 'promting questions' that reveal the students' thinking and the ways they made the links, and, 'debriefing interviews' that described what the students did while reading) that focus on ideas, words, and phrases that were taken from different parts of the same text plus their personal experience or their knowledge of the world; others exhibited features of intertextual relations that focus on ideas, words, and phrases that were taken from the given two or three texts plus the students' personal experience or world knowledge; and still others exhibited features of extratextual relations such as ideas, words, phrases etc. which were primarily based on students' personal experience or knowledge of the world with least attention to or ignoring the given texts from which they were expected to synthesize. The investigation was on comprehension, not on writing. So it does not indicate organization of texts, paraphrasing words and sentences and integrating citations and documenting sources. It is not specific on what was to be selected and what was actually selected. The investigation does not clearly indicate specific criteria for ranking the comprehenders into three groups except the general features of intratextual, intertextual and extratextual relations.

Wang (1992) considers a broad scope of the term "intertextuality." He states "...intertextuality not only includes identifiable prior codes and conventions that help to ensure and constrain the production of meaning, it also incorporates unconscious signifying practices and lost intertexts that undergo infinite dissemination into other unidentifiable intertexts" (28). In this case, we may deal with the difficulty of specifying identifiable texts through direct quotations, paraphrasing, or commentary but the difficulty remains with 'other unidentifiable texts.' Wang (1992) does not indicate whether these 'other unidentifiable texts' refer to segments of a newly created text, or to what Kristeva (1980) considered 'mnesic traces' (memories), or Hartman's (1992) personal experience or world knowledge which cannot indicate their manifestation in the new text because they are not demonstrable.

Fairclough's (1992) view of intertextuality seems relevant to this issue. He states : "Intertextuality is basically the property texts have of being full of snatches of other texts which may be explicitly demarcated or merged in, and which the text may assimilate, contradict, ironically echo, and so forth" (82). It seems difficult to demonstrate what has been merged in because it is integrated with the writer's stored knowledge which is outside the given text or texts for a given task.

Fairclough (1992) also distinguishes three typological 'modes' of intertextual relations such as (1) 'sequential intertextuality' which refers to segments of texts that alternate within a single text; (2) 'embedded intertextuality' in which segments of one text are merged within the structures of another text; and (3) 'mixed intertextuality' in which segments of texts are joined in almost inseparable manner (118). I feel similar or more complex typological modes can emerge in the analysis of written essays. I have found these typological differences relevant to my investigation which also examines intertextual links made by the subjects when they synthesized their new texts.

Heyes and Tierney (1982) investigated the intertextual connections between the specific content of two texts and they found out that relevant topics or general knowledge play a determinant role in comprehending and learning new texts. Prior knowledge of similar texts on a given topic fosters interpretation or understanding of texts to enable the writer to write using sources because it facilitates reactivation of other texts which the writer has already read. Cairney (1990) also investigated how previous textual experiences affected the reading and writing of 6-12 year olds. He collected data through interviews on how the child wrote a story and he found out that seven major types of responses emerged. The child's story (as reported) showed one or more features of the following types of responses. They are : 1. use of genre, 2. use of character or strong characterization, 3. use of specific ideas without copying plot, 4. copying plot with different ideas/events, 5. copying plot and ideas, 6. transferring content from expository to narrative, and 7. creating a narrative out of a number of narratives (481). His study seems to invovle extratextual relations based on the children's experience or knowledge stored in their memories. His study does not include intratextual and intertextual relations. Neither does it indicate demonstrable links in which the children prove their ability to synthesize from given texts.

According to Summerfield (1992), intertextuality is the intersection, interconnection and interaction of texts with other texts. He also indicates how writers are immersed in reading various types of texts that can help them create new texts. It is true watching one movie reminds us of the plot, the characters, setting, theme, background music and so on of other movies as Summerfield points out. Summerfield does not specifically discuss any of the three dimensions of intertextuality. He expresses a general view that what children read shape and reshape their writing because their stored knowledge interacts with texts they read. Similarly, Short (1992) sees intertextuality as the process of making connections and interpretations of texts by referring to previous texts. In his study, he found out that first grade children synthesized texts similar to texts previously discussed by the group of children in the class. The connections were made to some unidentifiable sources because the ideas were integrated in the synthesizers'/children's minds. It is useful to encourage children to share what they have read, heard, listened or observed. Engaging in class discussion helps learners see the connections among texts and it broadens their horizon of world knowledge. Thus, teaching students to write from sources may help them to understand texts from different perspectives and to establish links among texts so that they may develop divergent views. Engagement in creating new texts from sources may ensure the importance of their contribution in creating knowledge.

Lemke (1992) recognizes patterns of intertextuality based on topical content, point of view toward audience and genre structure (259). He explains that the more the patterns of intertexuality are involved in a text, the greater the ease of interpretation. He also sees that intertextuality connections differ in degree and kind. The investigation related to patterns of intertextuality is crucial to the teaching/learning processes because it provides teachers and students with the opportunity to select teaching materials which are similar in most respects. These types of teaching materials facilitate the link between previously acquired knowledge and the new knowledge aimed at to be learned. Bloome and Egan-Robertson (1993) consider the location of intertextuality primarily in the text and the reader in literary studies, in language in social semiotic perspectives, in students as readers and writers in educational studies and in social interactions in a social construction. They studied a 15 minute first-grade classroom reading and writing lesson. The lesson was a discussion of a story read in the previous lesson. They analysed the data primarily of three children. Among other findings, they found out that the students' role in establishing intertextual links was not appreciated by their teacher and that the social construction of intertextuality generates links between local events and social, cultural and political contexts. Likewise, Hartman (1995) discusses how linguists, literary theorists and theologians locate intertextuality in the text as a material object; how literary theorists, and cognitive psychologists locate it in the reader as a material being; how literary theorists, cognitive psychologists, and semioticians locate it in the writer as a material being; how sociolinguists locate it in the context as a material milieu and how linguists and semioticians locate it in language as a material implement. He also discusses how different approaches connect cognitive, social, cultural, historical, linguistic, and semiotic production apparatuses to mechanisms or processes by which intertextual links are made. Different approaches associated these production apparatuses with, for instance, cognitive production with the mind, social production with social interactions among people, cultural production with artifacts, values and assumptions, political production with power relations, historical production with inherited norms and conventions, linguistic production with features of spoken and written language, and semiotic production with systems of signs. These apparatuses are responsible for extracting, constructing, creating and building meanings. He also sees "disciplines, professions, institutions and individuals" (525) as control or regulatory systems of intertextuality. In relation to the time during which intertextuality is observed and studied, he recognizes retrospective occurrence and on-line occurrence (adapted : 523-26). Hartman discusses different approaches or perspectives of creating texts. This thesis seeks to investigate whether teaching how to make intertextual links can help some social science and natural science students in reading and writing lessons for academic purposes.

Leinhardt and Young (1996) also studied how two historians who read one familiar text and another unfamiliar text use their field specific and general knowledge of history. In this case, familiar texts facilitate access and reactivation of prior knowledge or world knowledge of the reader. The reader looks for organizational relations, content relation, or genre structures which can foster interconnections between texts which he/she has read. The reader of unfamiliar texts is expected to establish knowledge about the texts which may serve him as an anchor for other similar texts. Developing stored knowledge about unfamiliar texts may require more time and more concentrated efforts but it may be worth doing it because meaningful learning is believed to be associated with integrated and stored knowledge.

As to the importance of the intertextuality in education, Hartman investigated the interextual links of eight proficient readers reading multiple texts in a two and a half to three hours session for each student over three weeks. Conducting the investigation outside the classroom context and the small number of participants are some of the limitations of his study. The participants were native language university students. The students were not expected to produce written texts and so his study does not indicate how students can organize their texts, select ideas, paraphrase words, sentences and paragraphs, integrate citations, and document sources. As to the significance or importance of constructing intertextual connections, Lemke (1992) states, "The social practices by which a community constructs intertextual ties between texts are of fundamental concern for text semantics, discourse analysis, and the study of social systems generally as well as for educational research" (258). Intertextuality is useful in classroom setting especially in teaching and learning reading and writing skills. In relation to the need for research, Bloome and Egan-Robertson (1993) point out that the use of intertextuality "in analysis of classroom reading and writing events has been limited" (307). This indicates that more research is required to understand how intertextual links are made during reading and writing lessons especially in second language classrooms.

Works Cited

Ackerman, J. 1991. "Reading, Writing and Knowing : The Role of Disciplinary Knowledge in Comprehension and Composing." *Research in the Teaching of English* 25 : 133-77.

Bakhtin, M.M. 1986. *Speech Genres and Other Late Essays*. Ed. C. Emerson and M. Holquist. Trans. V.W. McGee. Austin : U of Texas P.

Cairney, T. 1990. "Intertextuality : Infectious Echoes from the Past." *The Reading Teacher* 43 : 478-84.

Fairclough, N. 1992. "Discourse and Social Change." Cambridge, MA : Polity.

Fillmore, C.J. 1985. "Linguistics as a Tool for Discourse Analysis." Ed. T.A. Van Dijk. *Handbook of Discourse Analysis*. Vol. 1. London : Academic Press.

Greene, S. 1993. "The Role of Task in Academic Thinking through Reading and Writing in a College History Course." *Research in the Teaching of English*. 27 : 46-75.

Hartman, D. 1992. "Intertextuality and Reading : The Text, the Reader, the Author, and the Cotext." *Linguistics and Education*. 4: 295-11.

——. 1994. "Intertextual Links of Reader Using Multiple Passages : A Post-modern/ Semiotic/Cognitive View of Meaning Making." Ed. R.B. Ruddell, et al. *Theoretical Models and Processes of Reading* (4th ed.). Newark : International Reading Association.

——. 1995. "Eight Readers Reading : The Intertextual Links of Proficient Readers Reading Multiple Passages." *Reading Research Quarterly*. 30.3 : 520-60.

Hayes, D.A. and R.J. Tierney 1982. "Developing Readers' Knowledge Through Analysis." *Reading Reseach Quartely*. 17 : 256-80.

Kristeva, J. 1980. *Desire in Language : A Semiotic Approach to Literature and Art. Trans*. Thomas Gora, et al. New York : Columbia UP.

Leinhardt, G&K Young. 1996. "Two Texts, Three Readers : Distance and Expertise in Reading History." *Cognition and Instruction*. 14.4 : 441-86.

Lemke, J. 1992. "Intertextuality and Educational Research." *Linguistics and Education*. 4 : 257-67.

Neusner, J. 1987. *Canon and Connection : Intertextuality in Judaism*. Lanham : UP of America.

Roudiez, L.S. 1980. "Introduction." *Desire in Language : A Semiotic Approach to Literature and Art*, by J. Kristeva. Trans. Thomas Gora, et al. New York : Columbia UP.

Short, K. 1992. "Researching Intertextuality within Collaborative Classroom Learning Environment." *Linguistics and Education*. 4 : 313-33.

Summerfield, J. 1992. *Negotiations : A Reader for Writers*. New York : McGraw-Hill.

Wang, J. 1992. *The Story of Stone : Intertextuality, Ancient Chinese Stonelore, and the Stone Symbolism of Dream of the Red Chamber, Water Margin, and the Journey to the West*. Durham : Duke UP.

16

English for New Competencies

V.D. Singh

ELT needs to go beyond English to meet the new demands being made on it.

The main argument in this paper is that in the present era of information technology revolution and globalization, ELT in India needs to resuscitate itself to meet the "challenges ahead." Much traditional practices of ELT are in a moribund state as they seem to show little awareness of changing needs and demands.

A case in point relates to the choice of language skills given priority in the English curriculum. Largely (though not exclusively), following the recommendations made by the Education Commission (1964-66), reading comprehension was given a prime place in our English curricula, perhaps justifiably if we take into consideration the needs-perception of those days. The academic climate in English studies was strongly in favour of asserting the importance of language skills, which it was claimed was not fostered by the kind of literary studies generally pursued then (and perhaps even now). It is interesting to note that the arguments then advanced in favour of giving importance of the skills of reading were almost the same as we seem to support nearly four decades later. And they are for taking cognizance of such exigencies as caused by science and technology (currently in a little wider sense) and the desirability of aligning education with national needs. Needs change with changing times. Accordingly, curriculum renewal should be an ongoing process.

Though reading comprehension and study techniques continue to be an important skill to be acquired in English, forces of technological and economic change have made equally if not more important the acquisition of oral skills in the language. The failure of the traditional university courses to respond to this need and accommodate the teaching and testing of oral skills in the syllabi has led private enterprise to overtake mainstream education. Privately owned and run institutions have sprung into parallel channels. It is true that school and college curricula provide General Purpose teaching of English, and what private institutions cater to are Specific Purpose needs. But should our schools and colleges remain insensitive to what people want? Teaching of spoken English can certainly find a more important place in their curricula, and after the secondary stage courses should diversify to respond to the specific needs of the students. Instead what is happening is that the traditional, mainstream university courses in English language continue more or less to be what they were, and to meet new requirements some universities are conducting short to medium duration, part-time, ostensibly specific purpose courses. There might remain a distance between what actually get taught and the goal(s) of the course.

What are the traditional English language courses at the undergraduate level? They are usually structured as sketched below :

(a) a textbook consisting of selected passages in prose, and sometimes a few poems also, language exercises in comprehension, usage and composition follow each passage/ poem.

(b) a long text, usually a novel, a classic, simplified and/or abridged, or in its original form, for rapid reading.

(c) standard points of grammar and usage—narration, verb and tense usage often including phrasal verbs, sentence structure, articles, preposition usage, idioms, etc.

Examination and evaluation follow a two-paper division with a minimum pass requirement of 33%. A conclusion to be drawn from this practice, rather cynically, could be that it would be all right if a person with a Bachelor's degree with compulsory English was proficient in it to the extent of 33 per cent. Teaching, as is well known, follows a lock-step procedure, which is least conducive to fostering communicative abilities in the language.[1]

But the point of immediate interest here is not just the modes of teaching or examination. The point of interest is as to what extent the English curricula have or are responding to the new demands being made on them by the forces of IT revolution and globalization. Therefore what needs to be noted about the existing courses is that only a particular set of abilities are targeted. They are largely the abilities that are aimed at 'reading' and producing correct forms of the language in writing. Skills of oral communication, to the extent they are acquired, are acquired incidentally through engagement in the processes of listening to classroom lectures and learning formal/functional grammar, reading, and writing.[2]

We get an idea of the new demands from the following :

(1) the specification or expectation of language abilities in English for/from candidates for a variety of new jobs created outside the traditional domains of government employment;

(2) the supply in the form of new courses, classes, and course materials (made by privately motivated enterprise) pushed to the fore by market forces.

The skills that appear to be most in demand are those of oral communication. This probably is a matter of common knowledge. What needs to be pointed out however is that this obvious-looking need is almost always related to a purpose which requires a specialised practice of the oral skills. Rajinder Singh made a study of the oral communication needs of salespersons in direct selling situations (see reference below). He made audio-recordings of salespersons' (N 10) first encounters with prospective customers of the commodities or services they were appointed to canvas for. This recording of the on-the-job communicative performance is part of a fuller study in which were contacted 40 salespersons mostly graduates and beginners in the job of selling, 10 sales trainers and 10 customers. What emerges from an analysis of the triangulated data shows directions for ELT in India or specific purposes.

There were two questionnaires administered to the salespersons to know how they assessed their own ability in spoken English, and what they considered to be the important communicative functions they would need to perform during sales encounters.

Sales trainers were asked to express what *they* considered to be the salespersons' salient communicative needs in English. And finally the customers, who were interviewed and also responded to a questionnaire, were asked to say what they perceived the salespersons' discourse to be like and what their expectations from sales-talk were.

Not surprisingly, they all rate persuasiveness in sales-talk to be its chiefest merit.

Salespersons were of the view that their communication skills (along with the product quality) were the two more important factors that facilitated sales. Within communication skills, they identified the ability to convince, and next to it presentation skills to be the crucial ones. Further, they identified three skills they needed to be trained in :

negotiating in English,
socialising in English, and
interpersonal skills.

The highlighting of the above mentioned skills should not give the impression that the salespersons had either a high degree of linguistic control over English or they were complaisant about it. They were conscious of their limitations in this regard — knowledge of English grammar, usage, and pronunciation. But these were only secondary to communication skills although necessary for achieving them. The relationships and the priorities are clear. Better English was needed to persuade customers and to build rapport with them.

Sales trainers also rate higher interactional functions (*e.g.*, negotiating, persuading) in salespersons' on-the-job communicative functions than transactional ones (*e.g.*, greeting, introducing).

On their part, the customers too rank communication skills as the most important factors that induce them to buy. At the same time they (9 out of 10) felt that salespersons needed to acquire improvement in the skills of effective listening. Most customers felt salespersons needed to improve their skills in negotiating and organizing their ideas logically and coherently, in addition to using appropriate words and expressions.

The conclusions are unmistakable. Effective sale-talk is not a simple matter of producing linguistically (grammatically and phonologically) correct English. Correct English is necessary but not enough. Unfortunately most courses and teaching materials on English when examined carefully give the impression that what one needs in order to be an effective user of English is to learn correct English. Courses on spoken English have stressed segmental and suprasegmental accuracy often to the exclusion of pointing out that spoken English is also a matter of an ongoing negotiation of meaning — a process with unforethought of turns and twists. To steer smoothly through this open-ended process one needs training in appropriate discourse abilities, and strategic competence.

Most courses on spoken English build language practice along familiar situations — at the railway station, in a book shop, etc. The dialogues according to a pre-written script as in a play. Natural real time communication, as we know, requires not only the resources of language but also a complex of other social and cognitive skills. Language abilities — higher the proficiency in them the better it is — form the base for this interplay. Learners need them, but going beyond them they need those other, special, kills which employers in the present-day context would look for.

Communicative language teaching is certainly making amends for some of the shortcomings of the traditional, accuracy-oriented teaching. But it prepares learners mainly for general communication. Going beyond this ELT needs to become ESP as in the case of language/oral communication needs of the salespersons. The implications of this observation appear to be that ELT in the present era, when face-to-face with new professional needs has to have an interface with other disciplines — psychology, salesmanship, etc. Otherwise how does one learn to persuade?

Notes and References

1. This critique of General English courses is not intended to be little in any way the usefulness of general purpose proficiency courses. They are necessary and act as foundations on which both advanced level and specialised courses are built. To what extent the General English courses achieve the goal of developing among the students general communicative proficiency/fluency is an altogether different consideration.

2. Of course the UGC has made a concerted move to introduce vocational courses, and the vocational version of the degree level English is what it first chose to call "communicative English" and later christened "functional English." The version of the syllabus for the spoken English component as originally recommended by the UGC was a despair. Still, even if we have an ideal syllabus, how do we ensure that it would be translated in the classrooms across the country in manners that are maximally conducive to the professed aims of the course.
3. It is to be noted that curriculum change is not a simple matter of just specifying syllabus content as isolated entity. Teacher training and teacher readiness to implement the syllabus are one among many other factors, which work together synergically.

Rajinder Singh, 1998. An analysis of salespersons' oral communication needs in English during sales encounters. (Ph.D. dissertation submitted at CIEFL, Hyderabad).

17

Re-Structuring English and Challenges Ahead

Chandrashekhar B. Sharma

Even in this age of Science and Technology, life remains a mystery eluding all attempts to define it in final terms. Therefore, there are expressions like 'change is the spice of life', 'Change is the essence of life' and "Life wells up alters and adds." But this much is almost true that science and its gifts have brought so many startling changes in the even tenor of life, that it seems more appropriate to say that the modern man is living in the age of Scientific Revolution.

When something is subjected to the process of revolution, it either experiences anomalous growth or too much of emaciation; but finally both result in the death and destruction of life. It seems, modern man is passing almost through a similar phase. Being ever reinforced with the inventions and discoveries of science and technology, he is leaping with a giant stride. Consequently everything invented by him, becomes outdated and obsolete just after the expiry of a short period of time like five to ten years. However, this is to the advantage of mankind because it enriches him ever as it leads to accumulation of knowledge and information. In brief the "Information Explosion" is on, during the present century. In this respect the following comments seem pertinent :

> It is estimated that 85 to 90 per cent of the scientists of all time are now living, an indication of the accelerated growth of knowledge and information in recent years.[1]

In order to benefit the entire globe with the latest information and accumulated knowledge, attempts are always on to evolve the finest and quickest means of communication. Language plays a pivotal role in the process of communication. With its help, man passes on his thoughts and feelings to another man or to his community, while carrying out his daily activities and chores. In the light of this fact, it is imperative on a man's part to know not only the past of the language he uses but also about its present condition. A.C. Baugh makes a pertinent remark in this context :

> But it is reasonable to assume that the liberally educated man should know something of the structure of his language, its position in the world and its relation to the other tongues, the wealth of its vocabulary together with the sources from which that vocabulary has been and is being enriched, and in general the great political, social, and cultural influences which have combined to make his language what it is.[2]

So far as English is concerned, it had a humble origin as the language of the lower classes just after the Norman Conquest. But in course of time it kept on flourishing and now it has acquired an international status. It is spoken in more than a quarter of the area of the globe. It means it is on the way of ascendancy. It is not only the language of the mighty British who once held sway over a large part of this globe but also of the modern super power i.e., the U.S.A. which initially acquired it from the British Colonists during early seventeenth century. Now the U.S.A. has emerged as the unquestioned super power in respect of military, economic, political and modern cultural life. Even numerically this language has the largest speakers in the international arena. Its supremacy in the international field is almost unquestioned. Quite long back, once John Galsworthy speculated in the following lines :

> Any impartial scrutiny made at this moment of time must place English at the head of languages as the most likely to become in a natural unforced way, the single intercommunicating tongue.[3]

The future of a language largely depends on the political, economic and cultural assertiveness of its users. In the light of this statement, the future of English seems very bright. Even the countries like China, Germany, and Russia are promoting the education of this language in order to meet the international requirement of their countries, in the age of Information Technology. So are doing most of the Gulf countries. The roots of this language are getting deeper in the Indian soil which decided long back to have Hindi as its official language. To a small section of the Indian population, it is like their mother tongue. Particularly after the sixties there has been a creative upsurge in the field of Indian writing in English. Similarly, we come across a different genre of African English. It means the popularity of English is gradually increasing. As a result, instead of one English, the present age has many Englishes. This is something like a happy/unhappy phenomenon. All the users of English, specially linguists and teachers are required to pay special attention to stem the rot. Actually any sort of disintegration should be depreciated because it has a weakening effect on the primary source. If the mushroom growth of Englishes is not checked, English will lose its significance as the most scientific language of the world. This seems to be the most difficult task because every nation enjoys the right to use English to express its ethos, culture and sensibility in the most befitting manner. But at the same time, it is expected that it must not distort the basic spirit of the language i.e., exactness, clarity, logicality and coherence.

Every English has convincing arguments in its favour to justify its separate existence. As for example, the American English has greater uniformity in respect of pronunciation and spellings. It generally tends to do away with most of the inflections while trying to attune the spelling of words to their pronunciations. But it has a slight leaning to the archaic usage of some words. On the other hand, the British English nurtures a scientific spirit in respect of the spellings of words. It always tries to bring into currency such words which sufficiently meet the demand of the time. It does not hesitate to discard archaic usage of words. But in respect of pronunciation, there is not so much uniformity among the British inhabitants of different localities. There is no corelation between the spelling and pronunciation of a large number of British words. Similar is the problem in respect of stressing or unstressing syllables or syllables between the British and American speakers.

To be exact, there are merely apparent differences between the

British English and the American one. R.N. Roy's comments in this respect seem pertinent :

> For, English of England and the English of United States are one language though during the three centuries, since the first settlements in America each has developed divergences in vocabulary, grammar, pronunciation and spelling.[4]

Above all the British English enjoys cultural superiority over the American English because the former has the likes of Shakespeare and Milton of whom the latter will hardly think of in ages to come. However, this does not mean the denigration of the literary achievement of American English writers. It simply aims to suggest that the British are richer and rather older in cultural aspect. But the other essentials for the survival of language are there with Americans. Actually this type of analysis would not be able to meet the demand of the modern world which seems to shrink in respect of size due to the various gifts of science and technology. It would not be unjust to say that the dimension of time and space is ever on shrink. The dream of 'World State', now, does not seem to be a distant reality. The North and South Koreas have merged their separate identities, so have the East and West Germany. Above all, eleven European countries have recently brought into usage a common currency. The disintegrated Russian Republics are once again on their move to stand united. If all these things have become possible, there is no doubt that all the Englishes could be one in near future, if teachers and linguists sit together to universalize this language by removing certain anomalies in respect of its usage, spelling, pronunciation, coinage of words and so on. If a language fails to adapt itself to the demand of the time, it is doomed to perish. It is happy that the Information Technology which is playing a universalizing and unifying role in this age. It has taken into its fold the fields of Science, Technology, Trade and Commerce, Transport and Communication and so on and so forth. America being the natural leader in these fields, it can play a decisive role in meeting the various challenges which seem to be imminent in the field of English language. But while doing so, it should try to preserve the separate cultural identity of the users of the language because a country gets enslaved forever if its cultural values are subjected to invasion and demolition. The English teachers are also required to be vigilant in this re-structuring and re-fashioning the syllabi of universities and colleges. Due to faulty and rather defective formation and pursuance of English syllabi, a kind of non-seriousness and rather depreciable sophistication is taking place among the Indian students. This gets reflected in the thin attendance in the classes and their greater dependence on cheap and spurious market notes. To me, an effective, dynamic and growing language is able to communicate in the fewest possible words without harming the sense, meaning and message in the most direct and clear way. This fact should be borne in mind while re-structuring English syllabi to meet the demand of the electronic media, industry, trade and commerce.

Notes and References

1. Robert G. Murdick, Joel E. Ross and James R. Collagett. *Information Systems for Modern Management* (New Delhi : Prentice-Hall India, 1995) 11.
2. Albert C. Baugh, *A History of the English Language* (New Delhi : Allied Publishers, 1991) 1.
3. Baugh 8.
4. R.N. Roy, *A Short History of the English Language and English Phonetics* (Caltutta : A Mukherjee & Co., 1989) 94.

18

Multi-media Approach to the Teaching of English through the Distance Mode

C. Goverdhan

Distance Education (D.E.), when compared with the conventional face to face system of education, is very young. In fact it is an off-shoot of conventional education but with its own distinct characteristics. When it comes to the question of instruction, unlike the conventional education system, it uses the multimedia approach in teaching. Apart from the printed material it extensively uses electronic media in imparting education to its distant learners who are scattered all around. Thus D.E. is quick in adopting the phenomenal changes in information technology revolution.

In computing, microelectronics and telecommunications new materials, systems, tools and techniques are being invented at an astounding rate. The three in combination offer opportunities to impart education. So it is for us to make use of it in the area of English language teaching (ELT) as there is a greater potentiality for everyone of non-native speakers of English who wish to learn fast. ELT can make use of the devices and systems belonging to the new technology ranging from Cyclops *i.e.,* Audio-Visual tutoring by phone, Videodisc, Video Casette, Videotext, teletext, satellites and fibre optic cable to pocket calculators, mainframe computers, microcomputers and cable and open circuit television.

In advanced countries there is a greater availability of the much sophisticated technology and the same is being used by them in spreading the education. But in India, the Distance Education

Institutions are gradually adopting what is feasible to our Indian conditions. Dr. B.R. Ambedkar Open University, Hyderabad is broadcasting the programmes through radio, which is a less expensive medium and can effectively reach distance learners in remote area. IGNOU, New Delhi is telecasting its programmes through Doordarshan. The continued use of radio and television by the Open Universities speak of the effectiveness of this media. Further, IGNOU developed audio and video cassettes which act as substitutes of radio and television as the broadcast timings may not be suitable to all the learners. But much needs to be done to improve these programmes. In fact, they are the reproduction of what is present in the Foundation Course in General English. In this regard, an innovative teacher of English can make the programme more interesting and interactive, keeping in view the specific needs of the distance learners.

Further daily news papers can also be used to teach English to the distance learners. All of us know that on every Tuesday "The Hindu" newspaper carries a very popular box item titled "Know your English." In a survey in Nirmal Town it was revealed that out of 100 subscribers 75% of them read this article. The respondents said that it arouses interest in them to learn more of English. So, on similar lines, it is suggested than the mass media like newspaper can be exploited by publishing certain items of grammar in news-paper corners for the benefit of the distance learners. They should also be given exercises and the answers of which may be published the next day.

Apart from the mass media like radio, television and news paper, the Distance Education Institutions can make use of the "Teleconferencing Services", telephone tutoring and computers. IGNOU arranges "Teleconferencing" from New Delhi to its Regional Centres spread throughout the country during the ten day contact programme of its students of P.G. Diploma in Higher Education. Through this special arrangement with satellite the learners located in Hyderabad can get their doubts clarified with the experts in New Delhi. The same can be availed by the learners of other Regional centres, as it is a live programme. Thus there is scope for exchange of knowledge and save time and travelling expenses. Audio, Video teleconferencing can be exploited further to impart education to the distance learners.

Another boon of information technology revolution, the telephone is also being used as a self-supporting aid in language education quite extensively especially in USA. Telephone tutoring has been used as a supplement to correspondence education in schools. It was reported by R. Flink in his 'Correspondence Education combined with systematic Telephone Tutoring (1978)', that in the Swedish experimental study of the use of telephone tutoring in the teaching of French, the group that had received telephone tutoring achieved higher scores than the control group when taking the final test. In India, the Distance Education Institutions should explore the possibility of clarifying the doubts of the distance learners through telephone by providing a schedule of availability of distance tutors. If such an arrangement comes into vogue, the distance learners can save their time and travelling expenses. It is not difficult to adopt as there is a fast growth of telephone system in the present Indian Society.

In addition to the above, the mainframe computers are being used in distance education from several years. Most of the Systems are used for marking tests, reporting results and marking statistical analysis. One such system is called CADE (Computer Assisted Distance Education). In this system the learners' assignments are scanned by an optical reader and the relevant comments are selected by the computer according to the profile of the results. IGNOU, New Delhi has adopted the above method of evaluating the assignments of some of its courses which it describes as 'Computer Marked Assignments.'

As regards computers, we are using the fourth and fifth generation ones. There has been a constant improvement. The second generation of CALL (Computer Assisted Language Learning) technology which is currently being developed, will be very helpful in the widespread use of it in second language (L2) learning. In advanced countries computer Assisted Instruction (CAI) has operated for many years on both mainframe computers and mini computers. The distance learners in countries like Australia, the UK and the USA with their personal computers are receiving the education through the facility of computer Assisted Instruction (CAI). In a distance test the learners received a computer generated proficiency profile with a description of their individual level in five different sectors of language proficiency *viz.*,

(a) Vocabulary.

(b) Oral production.

(c) Listening comprehension.

(d) Pronunciation.

(e) Written production.

The above instance shows, the immense role computers can play in ELT but in Indian context, the ground reality is that only the Government, Private Sector and the elite group possess the computers. Imparting education to the Indian distance learners through computers is not possible in the near future as most of them hail from underprivileged group and cannot afford a personal computer. So ELT through computers to the distance learners is a distant cry. But that does not mean that the computer programmes in ELT should not be developed.

Teaching through New Information Technology : Disadvantages

The new information technology which we want to use in ELT has its own disadvantages. When we prepare course material the students previous knowledge and needs should be taken into consideration. Thus a video tape may teach a topic in poorly related fragments among which important pieces are missing or it may be biased which goes uncorrected.

In the case of computers, the writers of computer courseware, many of them without training in Education and classroom experience, devise materials that may be elegant in terms of the use of computer technology but abysmal as teaching. Further, only fragments of the syllabus can be covered through using new information technology.

To conclude, now we have a new technology with great potential for ELT. We do not know enough yet about how to take full advantage of the technology, or about how to avoid the disadvantages. So the teachers of English should develop different devices and systems which should help the learners, particularly the distance learners in many ways.

Notes and References

1. Hawkridge, David. 1976 : *New Information Technology.*
2. Flink, R. 1978. *Correspondence Education Combined with Systematic Telephone Tutoring.*
3. Mehra, Masani. 1984. *Broadcasting and the People.* New Delhi : NBT.
4. Zetterson, Arne. 1986. *New Technologies in Language Learning.*
5. ——. 1995. *Communication Technology for Distance Education.* New Delhi : IGNOU.

19

Academic Writing and Intertextual Links

Tecle Ghebremuse

This research seeks to investigate some problems the students face in making intertextual links when they compose their own single text from three texts on a topic and to understand the nature of the intertextual links made by the subjects (students) in the study?

This research also tries to answer the following research questions.

(1) How do students in academic writing compose new texts?

(2) What problems do these student-writers face when they write using multiple sources on a topic?

Thus, the study has the following objectives :

(a) To identify the causes of the problems of student academic writing;

(b) To seek insight into the nature of intertextual links, and

(c) To suggest procedures whereby students can improve their academic writing.

Aims and Importance of the Study

The aim of the study is to explore innovative and practical approaches and to contribute empirical data to our knowledge of how English as a second language (ESL) student writers in particular and native language writers in general improve their academic writing ability. Hence, the study is hoped to be significant for :

(a) Providing student-writers with explanation of intertextual links and;

(b) Suggesting procedures for improving academic writing.

Academic writing and non-academic writing

In relation to two settings of writing, Anson (1988) distinguishes academic writing as "writing produced within educational institutions" and non-academic writing as "the writing in the world of industry, and corporate management, the government and public service agencies" (6).

Academic writing is a type of writing that is concerned with the teaching-learning process at school setting. Horowitz (1986) sees "summary of or reaction to a reading, annotated bibliography, report on a specified participatory experience, connection of theory and practice, case study, synthesis of multiple sources and research project" (449) as some categories of academic writing whereas non-academic writing refers to the type of writing that deals with writing outside school setting such as writing books and other prints for unspecified grade levels on, for instance, advertisement, production, management, exhibition, recreation, instruction, etc. Academic writing and non-academic writing share many common features of writing and they are interdependent. Although they reflect overlapping characteristics, researchers find it useful to make distinction between them for the sake of convenience in conducting research.

Odell and Goswami (1982) note that academic writing may have remote consequences as compared to non-academic writing. What is written in school setting is usually read by the teacher as audience as Odell and Goswami state that the teacher is "a person who may not expect to learn something he/she does not already know or have to his/her feelings, thoughts or actions influenced by the substance of writing" (202). Here, academic writing involves less effect of change in the reader's/audience's mind as compared to writing in non-academic writing. However, in non-academic setting, as Odell and Goswami point out, writing may have immediate consequences as in the case of job-related writings which affect one's promotion and salary increment as the writing induces change in the reader's/audience's mind. In relation to this, Nystrand's (1982) use of the phrase "writer's audience" refers to "the speech community of the writer." Nystrand states "writers may easily address readers they will never meet-even individuals who will be born long after they themselves have died" (15). This implies wide range of audience, along with wide range of purposes, mode of discourses, formats, stylistic variations of non-academic writing . Moreover, the writer expects to bring some sort of change to his audience through his/her writings.

Bridegeman and Carlson (1984) noted in their "survey of academic writing tasks" that their survey data show "that different disciplines do not uniformly agree on the writing task demands or a single preferred mode of discourse for evaluating entering undergraduate and graduate students" (279). This indicates diversity of writing in academic writing that require specified readers. However, Bartholomae (1985) referring to the novice in universities argues that writers have to know various skills such as "selecting, evaluating, reporting, concluding, arguing that define the discourse of our community" (134). Jolliffe and Brier (1988) also consider readers in academic writing as "intellectual community." Bartholomae, and Jolliffe and Brier's view on "the discourse of our community" or "intellectual community" is useful for the early stages of university education when the student is demanded to write to different professors in different departments. Detailed knowledge of an entire discourse of a university may be beyond the student writer's knowledge in a university. It seems logical to consider various genres of departments than to consider discourses of a university as a whole although departments share some common features of writing.

In academic writing as Applebee (1984) points out, textbooks selected by teachers at students' expected grade level are the primary sources of writing in school setting and it is expected that the textbooks serve as models for writing. Kennedy's (1985) findings corroborate this view. Kennedy noted that competent readers extract and incorporate information from sources better than less competent readers. Similarly, Nelson (1990) found out that resources, from which students draw information for academic writing, interact to shape their approaches. However, in non-academic writing, writing is usually initiated by the writer and it does not necessarily require information from books selected for readers at specific grade level.

In academic writing, the educational processes are strongly attached to power-relations. Consequently, the student writer is usually inclined to adopt the positions of the sources or his/her readers/teachers. McCarthy's (1987) findings with Dave, a case study, support this view of power-relation. McCarthy noted that Dave could not define "his own audience, purposes, or format" (261). This indicates that in school setting, the writer writes to reflect his/her socialization and adaptation to the group's or department's linguistic and socio-psychological conventions. Nevertheless, in non-academic writing, there is no clear and fixed point of reference and there may be loose power-relations between the writer and the audience/readers. In this case, the writer defines almost the criteria for effective writing from his/her prior knowledge, experiences, imagination, observations and creativity. Here, the writer has freedom to be critical or uncritical of his experiences, observations, imagination, abstraction, inferences and generalisations.

It is important to investigate how academic tasks, disciplinary conventions, and teacher-student relationships shape students' text production. The investigation can also help us to explain why some students simply reproduce the texts while others attempt to generate new ideas, infer or even argue for or against the ideas in given texts. So I would argue that students who know and use techniques of writing using several texts on a topic can improve their ability of producing new texts.

Academic Writing Using Multiple Sources

In academic writing using multiple sources, the writer uses texts to transform the contents and create new text. Professors at colleges and universities recommend several books for the courses they teach. Students are required to read, extract and store the gist of what they read in order to help them in answering examination questions in which the sources are unidentifiable because the gist of their contents is completely integrated into their prior knowledge. The students may also be required to write notes, lab reports, expository or argumentative essays, critical papers, research papers and so on in which the sources are usually identifiable from the citation and paraphrasing. Thus, writing using multiple sources is an indispensable type of writing especially at the tertiary level. It is a skill worth developing and mastering because it plays a significant role in the academic life of students at tertiary level.

Writing using multiple sources is an extremely demanding activity which involves thorough understanding of the gist of the content, ability to identify essential information, ability to extract and then connect new knowledge from sources with prior knowledge stored in long-term memory, ability to create organizational structures appropriate to the newly created text which may be synthesized from the organization of sources incorporated into the organizational principles of the writer's prior knowledge, and ability to manipulate language in terms of appropriacy and correctness.

Theoretical Background

Teaching writing using multiple sources approach (TWUMSA) especially at an undergraduate level involves the use of L2 readings as sources for ideas in creating new texts. I believe that in suggesting ways of improving sophomores' academic writing ability, cognitive interactionist as well as cognitive constructivist approaches involve and extend process-based as well as student-based approaches to writing in which a technique known as TWUMSA can be usefully employed. It involves operations and activities such as understanding and organizing texts, selecting, generating and connecting ideas, paraphrasing, and integrating citations and documenting sources. These operations and activities seem to play vital roles in improving writing ability for academic purposes at advanced or tertiary level especially for those who are expected to write in English as a second or foreign language.

Thus, this study seeks to provide insight into major factors affecting academic writing using multiple sources. It will explore how interactions among components of TWUMSA are reflected in the students' essays from three sources on a given topic, the intertexual links made by the students, and what composing strategies the students followed to accomplish their composing task.

Researchers such as Garner (1982), Brown, Day, and Jones (1983), Hare and Borchardt (1984), and Hidi and Anderson (1986) investigated the cognitive processes involved in summarizing texts by novice and expert summarisers. Their studies have extended the dimensions of investigative writing processes when they studied from the perspective of summarizing single texts.

The desire to extend the use of reading materials as models for teaching writing in general to using texts for developing operations or activities which seem indispensable to academic writing at tertiary levels motivated this study. In connection to this, Campbell (1990) considers integrating information from readings as a feature of successful academic writing. She also points out that integrating information from other texts has scarcely been directly studied in the writing of native as well as nonnative speakers of English. She also states "Even rarer is documentation of the highly complex processes followed by academic writers using background sources - processes that involve reading, understanding, learning, relating, planning, writing, revising, editing, and orchestrating" (211).

Referring to her study on *The composing Processes of College Students Writing from Sources* Kennedy (1985) says "The writing across discipline movement provided an impetus for this research, as did the recent paradigm shift in many composition courses from using correlated readings as models for teaching writing to using them as information sources for paraphrasing, summarizing and synthesizing" (436). She wanted to determine how student-writers at college level used assigned reading sources and she found out that competent readers use more strategies and they were more actively engaged in reading than less competent readers.

Concerning the role of arrangement of information in the writers' mind, Spiro *et al.* (1987) state "Coherent representation or configuration of meaning facilitates understanding and enables writers to access relevant strategies so that they can use what they know effectively" (48). When writers compose from sources, they search for connections among ideas which may foster mental representation of meaning as well as form which may be retrievable for use.

In connection to essay writing using passages, Newell and Winograd (1989) point out that activities such as "examining evidence and marshalling ideas, integrate the important information into their knowledge of the topic" (200). In this case, Newell and Winograd emphasize the processes of how new knowledge from sources incorporate into the existing knowledge of the writer during composing.

In relation to the process of constructing meaning from sources, Spivey and King's (1989) studies involve (hierarchical classroom setting of) 6th, 8th and 10th graders and one composing assignment from three descriptive texts on the same topic. The subjects produced their essays within three consecutive days. They examined mainly four composing variables such as quality of content, organization, connectivity and holistic quality. They found that the students who were not encouraged to include their own ideas inclined to depend on ideas from the source texts. Similarly, Spivey (1987) recognizes writing using source texts as the construction of composite mental representation which entails the connection of information from source texts and the writer's prior knowledge. In addition to this, Spivey's (1990) study involves 40 junior and senior university students who were given three encyclopaedia articles which provided the students with factual information on a single topic 'armadillos'. In this case, she describes the types of transformations made by the students in reference to the processes of organizing, selecting, and connecting information in writing from source texts. Referring to organizing, she states "...writers discover and invent relations as well as content units as they shape their mental representations and generate form for the texts they are creating" (265). Writing using source texts would invite and encourage writers to play an active role in transforming information from sources through creating (usually) a new organization, selecting salient points, paraphrasing author's ideas, and establishing connections among ideas. It may also inspire writers to contribute to the production of the new text by generating ideas from their existing knowledge. Connections made among ideas from the sources may also serve the writers as an anchor for future connection so that a network of interconnections may develop.

Flower *et al.* (1990), also consider reading to write as a literacy event in which the writer's knowledge of linguistic, rhetorical, and contextual awareness and strategies interact with different types of information available in source texts, the writer's experiences and learning, and the context for constructing meaning.

Ackerman's (1991) study includes forty graduate students from the Departments of Psychology and Business. The students were asked to write an essay that explained and showed their understanding of the nature and importance of one of two given topics from four passages for each topic. He stressed the importance of reading to write in order to construct a new mental and textual representation as ultimate outcome in comprehending and composing. Ackerman found that prior knowledge in reading to write plays an important role. He also found that the 'high knowledge' writers included more evaluative elaborations and new ideas in their essays than the 'low knowledge' writers. Referring to reading and writing he says "...a constructivist perspective generally assumes a cognitive interplay of prior and immediate ideas in the mental representation of composers" (135).

Greene (1993) investigated how different writing tasks affected student writers' composing from sources and she found out that the writers constructed different representations of meaning because report and comparison tasks seem to expect them to select, organize, and connect information differently (48). So, lecturers need to design writing tasks that can prepare students to meet their departments' expectations.

Hartman (1995) investigated the intertextual links of competent readers and he recognizes those readers (a) with many more links to endogenous [within the given texts) resources, (b) with links to both endogenous and exogenous [outside the given texts] resources, and (c) with many more links to exogenous resources.

Mayer (1992) recognizes learning as response acquisition, knowledge acquisition and meaning construction. Referring to learning as meaning construction from books, and lectures, he points out that selecting information, organizing new information and integrating the new knowledge from sources into existing knowledge play indispensable roles. In connection to the knowledge construction view, Mayer (1997) also says :

> "The underlying premise of cognitive constructivism is that humans actively build their own knowledge. Rather than being a commodity that can be transferred from one person to another, new knowledge is constructed within the context of one's existing knowledge. ...Cognitive processing involves active construction including selecting, organizing, and integrating knowledge" (479).

In relation to accessing existing knowledge, Franke and Grouws (1997) state "The connections between ideas enable an individual to search her mental structure, moving from connection to connection, in an attempt to gain access and combine information, so that it can be purposely put to use" (311). They also point out that individuals' successful search for their mental connections rely on types of information, manner of connections, and the strength of their linkage. An individual who is unable to gain access to a piece of information cannot use it.

All the above mentioned studies have some common features such as that they did not involve intervention (teaching or instructing students); they were conducted with native language student-writers in a native language environment; most of them were outside the classroom setting and they involved a small number of students, and data were mostly collected through think aloud protocols and different forms of interviews....

Taking this brief review into account, my study involves learners of English as a second language — strictly speaking English as a medium of instruction. It includes a large number of student-writers in a non-native English speaking environment. It also includes teaching some strategies to improve reading and writing. The reading and writing strategies include lessons on :

> understanding or interpreting sources, organizing texts, selecting ideas, generating ideas, connecting ideas, paraphrasing words, phrase, sentences and paragraphs, integrating citations and documenting sources when the subjects write in English as a second language.

So I want to investigate the academic writing of 112 university students who are learners of English as a second language in classroom setting and through their written performance using multiple sources. I shall investigate the intertextual links by locating intertextuality in the writer as a reader, in the cognition and on-line reading of the three texts or passages , on-line writing the new text and on retrospective occurrence in the interviews.

Procedures for Randomly Assigning Subjects to two Groups-Phase I, Gr. I.

In assigning the subjects in my study, I adopted the randomized pretest-posttest control group design which involves experimental and control groups, because firstly, the study demands that all the subjects in the experimental group be free at the same time. Secondly, the instructional materials and reading and writing tasks may be highly relevant and interesting to some and less relevant and uninteresting to others when subjects are drawn from about fifteen departments. Thirdly, it is extremely difficult if not impossible to find the required students who are willirg to serve in the experimental or in the control group for non-credit course for a semester (usually sixteen weeks). Fourthly, I wanted to include subjects from the departments of Social sciences such as Anthropology and Sociology, English and Law as well as from the department of natural sciences such as Plant Science and Soil and water Conservation in my study in order to understand the nature of academic writing in both sciences.

Students from the Departments of Language Studies (thirty-four), Anthropology and Sociology (twenty-five) and Law (fifteen) served in the study as experimental and control groups. These were the only groups of students who were required to take Sophomore English En 202. At first, they were assigned in three sections; however, it was realized that the students can be regrouped into two, assigning students into experimental group and control group randomly.

Instruction - Phase I

Experimental Group

Teaching Sophomore English En 202 through TWUMSA began by introducing the students to the ultimate goal, general content and the means to achieve the goal. The General purpose of the course was explained to the students that it was to improve their writing ability so as to prepare them for academic writing.

In designing the course contents, the subjects' knowledge, abilities, needs and motivation were considered. Information related to their actual studies was collected from their respective departments on the assumption that the subjects would be motivated if the course contents are related to their needs. The lecturer also tried as much as possible to make the subjects understand the relevance of what he was teaching to their other courses. So, the course contents were integrated into most of their subject areas. There were no previously used materials that reflect the approach.

Consequently, new materials — three texts on the same topic- were selected, typed, duplicated and distributed to the subjects every time they finished the writing task on a given topic throughout the semester. Lack of previously used instructional materials allowed flexibility and responsiveness to the new texts. Instruction emphasized teaching operations or activities such as how to understand and organize texts, how to select, generate and connect ideas, how to paraphrase words, phrases, sentences and paragraphs, how to integrate citations and document sources and how to summarize. Various types of discourses, bottom-up and top-down reading were also studied or treated. Exercises, quizzes and tests and writing tasks included thirteen topics (most of them three texts each).

In addition to this, the mid-semester and final exams included two reading passages on 'Social Class' and on 'Bringing up children' (respectively).

TWUMSA was employed to achieve the goal of preparing the subjects for academic writing: the types of academic writing required at tertiary levels such as *interpreting or understanding, analysing, synthesizing, and creating information as well as constructing meaning from source texts*. A holistic approach to the teaching of the components of TWUMSA was adopted because all the components could be demonstrated in a single text using multiple sources. In order to simplify instruction, emphasis was given to a particular operation or activity such as understanding the texts for two or three sessions and then moved to the next operations or factors. The operations seem to have 'horizontal relationships,' which do not require the mastery of one operation before moving to the next operation, rather than a 'hierarchical relationships,' which may require the mastery of one operation before moving to another operation. The method focused on the processes of composing an essay and it inspired the subjects to engage in discussion of how to produce essays relevant to their field of specialization

Control Group I

The students in the control group were learning writing in English according to the syllabus which seems to be based primarily on the current-traditional approach to writing. Course components are :

unit 1. revising and proof-reading written work, unit 2. composing a report, unit 3. practising how to take notes while listening to lectures, unit 4. seminar skills, Unit 5. Carrying out a survey, gathering data and presenting the results orally and in written form. In this case, the subjects' needs and motivation have not been fully considered.

The aims of the course seem too general. They may satisfy the needs of some students from some departments and almost ignore the needs of others, for example, biology, engineering, management students.

The handouts are not appropriate even for the minority of the students. And above all, the handouts do not require students to demonstrate knowledge of the handouts' content. So, writing without responsibility for the text content does not seem to correspond to writing for other academic courses. Writing tasks of this type may not engage students in composing texts in the way in which their respective departments require them to do. If students are not to benefit from what they study, the course needs to consider the students' needs and motivations and the connection of the course to other academic courses.

We can also understand from 'some suggestions for topic' that they do not have a direct bearing on their field of specialization.

In addition to this, the processes of reading/writing such as text marking, note-taking, organizing, planning, writing, revising, and feedback seem to be ignored

NB. Similar Procedures were Followed in Phase II-group II.

Subjects' Essays and Findings :

The origin of information whether it was drawn from the first, or the second, or the third, or combination of two or three or generated from the sources and the writer's existing knowledge was categorized. Each subjects' essay was parsed into content units in a modification of Ackerman's (1991) and Greene's (1993) procedures for analysing clauses in essays such as summary protocols.

In relation to understanding the texts, the subjects, especially in the control groups appear to copy exact more content units from the given source texts than the subjects in the experimental groups. This may suggest that the subjects had difficulties in understanding the contents of the texts to be able to write mostly in their own words. In connection to organizing which involves the introduction, the conclusion and paragraphing, the performance of the subjects in the experimental groups are better than the subjects in the control groups. Most of the subjects in the experimental groups included the introduction, and the conclusion, and they also showed better textual organization in paragraphing. As to selecting content units, the subjects in the control groups included a little more exact copying (verbatim) and paraphrased content units from the three texts than the subjects in the experimental groups. The subjects in the control group (phase I) included more (302) paraphrased content units (out of the grand total of 830 content units) than the experimental groups who included 265 paraphrased content units out of 940 grand total content units. In relation to generating new content units, the mean on generating content units of the experimental group (phase I) is significantly larger than that of the control group. This significant difference may be due the instruction given to the experimental group on the basis of teaching writing using sources. Concerning integrating citations and documenting sources, thirty-one of the control group (phase I) produced 294 exact copy content units without any acknowledgement to the sources used, whereas the experimental group produced 233 content units and twenty-eight subjects acknowledged their sources in 128 exact copy content units. Regarding connecting ideas from source texts as well as ideas from the texts and the subjects' existing or digested knowledge, the analysis of the subjects' essays reveals that the subjects in the experimental group are better than the subjects in the control. The experimental group's better results in connecting ideas we suggest are due to the effects of receiving instructions through TWUMSA.

In phase II, the control group produced 205 exact copy content units without any acknowledgement to the sources, whereas the experimental group produced 190 exact copy content units and seventeen subjects acknowledged the sources of 90 exact copy content units.

Intertextual Links

Intertextual links refer to the interaction, intersection and interrelationships among contents taken from source texts and generated contents from the sources texts and from prior knowledge of the writer as a reader. In relation to links, Mintzes et al. (1997) state :

The formation of links requires retrieving knowledge from long term memory (LTM), consciously interpreting, evaluating, comparing, and contrasting new information with prior knowledge, and ultimately reconciling and assimilating new information by subsumption [from less-inclusive to more general-unicellular to animals], and superordinate (from more general to more specific-radio waves to electro-magnetic energy) learning (422).

In this case, making links among ideas seems a complex process because it involves long term memory, prior knowledge and schematic knowledge.

The intertextual links made by the subjects in this study were manifested in various forms. In this connection, twenty seven of the subjects in the control group followed the sequence of the source texts in the task *i.e.,* linear or sequential arrangement of information. The subjects began composing using information from one text, then moved to the next text and then moved to his or her last text. Most of them started with the text on the first page and moved to the texts on the following passages consecutively *i.e* they started with the first and ended with the third source while few started with the text in the middle and moved either to the first or to the third text. The content units in their texts consisted of exact copy, paraphrased and generated CUs. The kind of intertextual links that starts with the first and ends with the last is to what Fairclough (1992) recognized as 'sequential' intertextuality in which "different texts or discourse types alternate within a text" (118). In this case, the content units from the three texts alternated within each student's essay. Five subjects made non-sequential intertextual links in which the writers started, for instance, with the first source, moved to the third, then to the first or second or third without any specific order. One subject used only two sources and he or she linked them without specific order. Another subject used only one source. Still another subject included only four paraphrased content units : three from the first and only one from the third. Almost all the content units composed by the last two subjects did not have any traceable orthographic phrase or sentence in the original texts. However, the meanings of the content units they composed seem to reflect the meanings in the three texts in general.

Concerning the experimental group, twenty-one, seven, and seven subjects started with the first, second, and third source texts respectively. Nineteen subjects followed non-sequential arrangement of information from sources while fourteen subjects followed sequential configuration of information from sources. Two subjects included exact copy Cus and paraphrased Cus only from the first source. Three subjects did not include exact copy or paraphrased content units from the third source; one subject did not include content units from the first, and still one subject did not include CU from the second. When we compare the intertextual links made by the control group and the experimental group, we can see that the intertextual links made by the experimental group appear more interwoven, interspersed and interconnected than that of the control group. These better intertextual links may lead to better integration of information from source texts as observed in this data analysis.

In phase II, twelve, four, and five subjects in the control group began with the first, second, and third sources respectively while twelve, two, and seven subjects in the experimental group started with the first, second, and third sources respectively. One subject in the control group and one subject in the experimental group composed their essays using only two source texts. The subjects in the control group began with the first sources and them moved to the second sources but he or she did not return to the first source; however, the subject in the experimental group began with the third source and moved to the first and again moved to the third, then to the first source freely.

Concerning the arrangement of information, in the control group eleven and ten subjects followed sequential and non-sequential configuration of information respectively while in the experimental group, sixteen and five subjects arranged their information non-sequential and sequential respectively. In this case, more subjects following non-sequential arrangement of information in the experimental group seems better at integrating information which might be the effect of TWUMSA.

Five kinds of Writers

Analysis of the subjects' essays reveals five kinds of student writers: those writers who merely transferred content units from sources text to their essays whom I recognize as "compilers" because they simply joined content units from sources; those writers who tried to maintain the balance between exact copy, paraphrased, and generated or reconstructed content units whom I recognize as "harmonizers", those writers who attempted to detach their essays from the surface structure of source texts and reconstructed essays whom I recognize as "reconstructivists," those writers whose essays consisted of mainly either exact copy and generated, or exact copy and paraphrased, or paraphrased and generated content units whom I recognize as "dualists" and those writers whose essays consisted of primarily paraphrased content units whom I recognize as " paraphrasers."

The "compilers" (12 subjects in the control and 6 subjects in the experimental groups) showed the least contribution to the content and surface structure of their essays, for instance, the writers of the following two excerpts included 84.85% (the first) and 100% (the second) content units in their essays.

In educational environment inter-disciplinary, need-based activities, inter-university, inter-institutional cooperation are required in identifying specific roles (SU4). As many developmental area have been identified (SU5), it would not be difficult for all the universities in a region to sit together and come to an understanding (SU6). This gives universities greater freedom and recognition of values of academic standard, merit and respect for excellence (SU10).

Earthworms usually remain near the soil surface (M7) but they are known to tunnel as deep as 2 m during period of dryness or in winter (M8).Earthworms also serve as fish bait (M17); hence the name angle worm and also provide food for a large variety of birds and animals (M10).

Here the writers presented somebody else' voices without much contribution to the content or form. These writers are similar to what Goffman (1981) recognized as 'animators' in a communication system. Referring to the submissive role of a reader Goffman (1981) states "In short, he [the speaker] is the talking machine, a body engaged in acoustic activity, or if you will, an individual active in the role of utterance production. He is functioning as an "animator" (144).This includes the writer who merely manifests somebody's content units without much involvement himself or herself in modifying or adapting the content. The writers in the examples above did not take any initiative to maintain logical coherence of their essays at least by using suitable cohesive devices, conjunctions, references, or substitutions. When the writers jump from content unit at one location to other content units at other locations in the same source text or in different source texts, it is likely that the essay will consist of isolated or fragmented content units. This is what happened with most of the essays especially in the control groups. Thus, it seems right to conclude that copying directly mostly others' content units may not enable the writers to improve their writing. The main issues are : Why did the writers composed their essays in such a way and how can we help them to liberate from such manifestations in their academic writing? Although it is difficult to specifically point out the primary causes, problems of understanding texts and lack of adequate ability to manipulate language structures may be the causes. In connection to why some students plagiarize, Hull and Rose (1989) concluded that some students plagiarized their essays when they felt they were expected to produce research papers in a language they might have barely mastered. In relation to plagiarism, Bloch and Chi (1995) state "...plagiarism may be a compensatory strategy used by novices just entering a field and experts well established in their discipline" (238). As to the remedy, Johns (1981) and Campbell (1990) recommended the teaching of strategies or operations such as paraphrasing, summarizing, quoting to ESL students to dissuade them from copying.

The "harmonizers" (13 subjects in the control and 20 subjects in the experimental groups) showed substantial contribution to the content and surface structure of their essays by restructuring and orchestrating the content from various sources and making use of some paraphrasing activities. For example, the writer of the following excerpt included 37.93, 34.48, 27.59 per cent exact copy, paraphrased, and generated content units respectively.

In this essay, I will try to deal with the role of higher education in the process of national development.(S), according to Apparaw, Joshi and Surdarsnam.

Higher education is a forward movement to change (S) and it needs new direction to meet its goals (A2+S). For example, the academic community is expected to play a leading role in these process of development and planning (A3). They should help in the extension of knowledge distribution in the community (S). In all developing countries the chance of getting knowledge, research and new skills have yet to reach to those people (A6) who are in need to it (A7). Of course, some parts of our contemporary world has reached a stage of highly advanced science and technology (S). So, there is a need of helping to develop for those societies (S) who do not reach these stage yet (S), by introducing appropriate technology; which is a means to promote individual and community self-reliance (A12) (Apparaw, 1980 : 14).

As can be seen from the above example, the writer sometimes included exact copy content units, and joined to other content units by adding some words at the beginning and/or at the end of the content units. Sometimes, he or she reconstructed almost half of the words of some content units. Here, the writer seems to make some sort of selection, addition of some cohesive devices, conjunctions and references to create harmony among the content units from sources and knowledge stored in his or her mind. He or she showed some transformations in the essays. Although the essay included exactly copied phrases in parts of the content units, the proportion of copied phrases and reconstructed phrases to form different content units appear almost balanced because included exact copy, paraphrased, and generated content units are in almost balanced proportion. As to the background of the writer at the University, he or she scored C, B, A, and B grades in the four English common courses. This may suggest that some above average or high scorers fall under this group.

The "constructivists" (4 subjects in the control and 7 subjects in the experimental groups) seem to show many integrated content units, if exact copy, paraphrased and generated content units represented integration of information along a continuum from the least integrated to the most integrated content units. Especially, coding content units as paraphrased or generated or reconstructed CUs is based on the features exhibited in the content units. So, there are some overlapping features at their boundaries. Here, the writers attempted to reflect the content of their source texts usually in their own words. They included added content units, cohesive devices, conjunctions, and substitutions but they did not engage in selecting content units from the sources that may serve them as frame of references. For example, the writer of the following excerpt included 80.95% generated content units.

As far as we know the world is to static(S). It is moving (S) and the problems are changing from time to time (S). So, the education system also has to move and change the ways of its approach for different movements and problems (S). Today the world is full of tremendous changing in technologies and social lives (S). It is moving fast, especially the developed countries such as America, China, Japan. To reach them, we underdeveloped/ developing countries have to run (S) when they walk (S). Otherwise we will be always behind them(S). Here, self-reliance is a good system for underdeveloped/developing countries (A12+S).

In this case, the writer tried to reflect the content of source texts. The shortcoming with "reconstructivists" as shown above is that there was observable detachment from the sources and the writer did not indicate whether he or she understood the sources by selecting and including exemplary content units, paraphrasing, integrating citations and documenting source of information they used in creating their essays. In this category, some extremists composed all the content units on their own words and content units. Some of them misinterpreted some content units in the source. Referring to arguing from sources, Kaufer and Geisler (1989) viewed "sources as enabling vehicle" (p. 297) for establishing one's position. So, one weakness of the writers in this category is that the writers did not make adequate use of sources to enable them to compose their essays.

In relation to one reader, Hartman (1994) states :

She [Dana] generated the highest proportion of *exogenous* intertextual links among the eight students. Nearly three-fourths of the textual resources she referenced were outside the task environment (71.4 per cent). In contrast, the group only referenced *exogenous* resources — two-fifths of the time (39.4 per cent). This strong tendency of hers not to transact with the passages in constructing a "textual world" suggests a *resisting* way of reading (632).

The above quotation indicates the criteria for grouping the readers in the study and some of the behaviours they exhibited when they read the sources texts.

Although it is very difficult to show the relationship between the writer and his or her essay, the writer scored four "C" grades in the four English common courses. This may indicate that some average scorers tend to generate content units considerably departed from the source texts in content and form.

The "dualists" (25 subjects in the control and 22 subjects in the experimental groups) produced at most below 64% and at least above 16% content units from any two of the three categories (Exact copy, paraphrased and generated CUs). Their essays consisted of either exact copy and generated, or exact copy and paraphrased or paraphrased and generated content units. The content units composed by these writers are exact copy and generated 2 and 6, exact copy and paraphrased 13 and 4 and paraphrased and generated content units for the control and experimental groups respectively. In most cases, the writers did not include enough content units from any of the third category. Their essays lacked either exact copy, or paraphrased or generated content units.

The "paraphrasers" (2 subjects in the control groups and 1 subject in the experimental groups) produced 93.33%, 70.83% and 68.18% paraphrased content units. Here, the writers could not demonstrate how to integrate citations and document sources. They could not also indicate whether they were able to generate content units from source texts and from knowledge stored in their minds. It is also difficult to observe their ability to interrelate content units.

Works Cited

Ackerman, J. 1991. "Reading, Writing and Knowing : The Role of Disciplinary Knowledge in Comprehension and Composing." *Research in the Teaching of English* 25 : 133-77.

Applebee, A.N. 1984. *Context for Learning to Write : Studies of Secondary Instruction*. Norwood, NJ : Ablex.

Bartholomae, D. 1985. "Inventing the University." Ed. M. Rose. *When a Writer Can't Write : Studies in Writer's Block and Other Writing Process Problems*. New York : Guilford.

Bloch, J., and L. Chi. 1995. "A Comparison of the Use of Citations in Chinese and English Academic Discourse." Ed. D. Belcher and G. Braine. 1995. *Academic Writing in a Second Language : Essays on Research and Pedagogy*. Norwood : Ablex Publishing Corporation.

Bridgeman, B. and S. Carlson. 1984. "Survey of Academic Writing Tasks." *Written Communication* 1 : 247-80.

Brown, A.L., J.D. Day, and R.S. Jones. 1983. "The Development of Plans for Summarizing Texts." *Child Development* 54 : 968-79.

Campbell, C.C. 1990. Writing with Other's Words : Using Background Reading text in Academic Composition. Ed. B. Kroll. *Second Language Writing : Research Insights for the Classroom*. Cambridge : Cambridge UP.

Fairclough, N. 1992. *Discourse and Social Change*. Cambridge, MA : Polity.

Flower, L., *et al.* Eds. 1990. *Cognitive and Social Processes in Reading to Write*. New York : OUP.

Garner, R. 1982. "Efficient Text Summarization : Costs and benefits." *Journal of Educational Research* 3 : 116-23.

Goffman, E. 1981. *Forms of Talk*. Oxford: Blackwell.

Greene, S. 1993. "The Role of Task in Academic Thinking Through Reading and Writing in a College History Course." *Research in the Teaching of English* 27 : 46-75.

Hare, V.C. and K M. Borchardt. 1984. "Direct Instruction of Summarizing Skills." *Reading Research Quarterly* 20 : 62-78.

Hartman, D. 1995. "Eight Readers Reading : The intertextual Links of Proficient Readers Reading Multiple Passages." *Reading Research Quarterly* 30.3 : 520-60.

Hidi, S., and V. Anderson. 1986. "Producing Written Summaries : Task Demands, Cognitive Operations, and Implication for Instruction." *Review of Educational Research* 56 : 473-93.

Horowitz, D.M. 1986. "What Professors Actually Require : Academic Tasks for the ESL Classroom." *TESOL Quarterly* 20.3 : 445-62.

Hull, G., and M Rose. 1989. "Rethinking Remediation : Toward a Social Cognitive Understanding of Problematic Reading and Writing." *Written Communication* 6 : 139-54.

Johns, A. and P. Mayes. 1990. "An Analysis of Summary Protocols of University ESL Students." *Applied Linguistics* : 253-71.

Jolliffe, D.A. and E.M. Brier. 1988. Studying Writer's Knowledge in Academic Disciplines. Ed. D.A. Jolliffe. *Advances in Writing Research Volume Two : Writing in Academic Disciplines.* Norwood : Ablex Publishing Corporation.

Kaufer, D.S. and C. Geisler. 1989. "Novelty in Academic Writing." *Written Communication* 6 : 286-11.

Kennedy, M.L. 1985. "The Composing Process of College Students Writing from Sources." *Written Communication* 2 : 434-56.

Mayer, R.E. 1997. "Incorporating Problem-Solving into Secondary School Curricula." Ed. G.D. Phye. *Handbook of Academic Learning : Construction of Knowledge.* San Diego : Academic Press.

McCarthy, L.P. 1987. "A Stranger in Strange Lands : A College Student Writing Across the Curriculum." *Research in the Teaching of English* 21: 233-65.

Mintzes, J.J., *et al.* 1997. "Meaningful Learning in Science : The Human Constructivist Perspective." Ed. G.D. Phye. *Handbook of Academic Learning : Construction of Knowledge*. San Diego: Academic Press.

Newell, G. and P. Winograd. 1989. "Effects of Writing on Learning from Expository Texts." *Written Communication* 6 : 196-217.

Nystrand, M. 1982. "Rhetoric's "audience" and linguistics' "Speech Community": Implications for Understanding Writing, Reading, and Text. Ed. M. Nystrand. *What Writers Know : The Language,Process, and Structure of Written Discourse.* New York : Academic Press.

Odell, L. and D. Goswami. 1982. *Writing in Non-academic Settings. Research in the Teaching of English* 16. 201-23.

Spiro, E., *et al.* 1987. Knowledge Acquisition for Application : Cognitive Flexibility and Transfer in Complex Content Domains. Ed. B.C. Britton. *Executive Control Process*. Hillsdale NJ : Erlbuam.

Spivey, N.N. 1987. "Construing Constructivism." *Poetics* 16 : 169-92.

___. 1990. "Transforming Texts : Constructive Processes in Reading and Writing." *Written Communication* 7 : 26-287.

Spivey, N.N., and J.R. King. 1989. "Readers as Writers : Composing from Sources." *Reading Research* Quarterly 24 : 7-26.

20

Second Language Acquisition (SLA) and the Computer Learner Corpus (CLC)

R. Subhashini and *Kesaraj Kumar*

1. An Overview

The onset of Computer Learner Corpus has been gradual. The language produced both in the spoken or written form by any non-English learner of English forms a collection of the corpus which can be used as the computer textual database. An effort has been made in this article to discuss various aspects related to this Computer Learner Corpus like, Corpus Linguistics and English Studies, Analysis of Learner Corpora, Vocabulary Frequencies in Advanced Learners' English, Overstatement in Advance Learners' Writing, Learner Corpora: Compiling ELT Dictionaries, Textbook Enhancement: A National Perspective and Empirically based Computer Assisted Language Learning (CALL).

The English Language Teaching Practitioners and the Second Language Acquisition specialists have started to recognize the theoretical and practical value of the learner corpora, and hence are gradually showing interest in it. They are responsible for promoting the fast growth by their contribution to the Learner Corpus in its formation and analyse. This is of a great significance to any Non-English learner of English as or English as a Second Language.

Not only in research but also in teaching, the database formed by the Computer Learner Corpus (CLC) is of a great use and informative too! For instance, in any Non-English, English speaking country like India, the English teacher deals with the subject almost every day or at least every week. And while doing so, the teacher often sets for the students some sort of assignments like comprehension or essays to write. After making the necessary corrections and comments, usually the material is returned to the students respectively. This process can form a Computer Learner Corpus if the teacher can save the assignments submitted by the students in his personal computer (PC). When this process of storing the assignments of the students is observed systematically and gradually at periodic intervals like week after week, forms a substantial collection of the student's (teacher's) performance. The data so collected and preserved in the computer forms the Learner's Corpus, that may form a basis or a source of information, in the light of which, the performance and progress of the students can be assessed and analysed at regular intervals and this provides a scope to study the progression or the improvement in the learning of the student to certain extent as a group activity. A highly useful data for research and teaching with various objectives can be drawn from this 'Corpus.' The different aspects that may be observed are follows:

(a) To study 'overused' (often repeated) and the 'under-used' (least repeated) linguistic features and the features that the learners of non-native speakers tend to observe than the native speakers do.

(b) To observe the learner's 'avoidance-strategies' and their scope of usage.

(c) The scope and extent of the learners (to be) in consonance with the native speakers of English.

(d) To assess the percentage of 'mother-tongue pull' effecting the learner in the acquisition of English.

(e) To make an estimate of the chief feature of a non-native learner's better and bad performance in the process of learning.

The above observations are useful both for the teacher and the taught by providing an insight to estimate the teacher's approach to the teaching of the language. This also facilitates for an immediate response of the students that may provide scope to anticipate or assess his students prospects in other institution in course of time, so also in other countries. If such parallel efforts are observed or followed by the teachers in other places and institutions that would provide an opportunity to evaluate more basic realities so as to realise certain questions like:

(a) To enlist the chief features that promote for the better performance of the learners in this country.

(b) The scope to counter the chief features that promote any bad performance in the process of learning can be estimated or evolved on research.

(c) This, in turn increases the scope for intensive, corrective and constructive research to promote speedy learning or acquisition of language.

2. Corpus Linguistics and English Studies

As the computers are becoming accessible day by day the computer corpus is also wide spread into all the related fields right from lexicography to literary criticism through artificial intelligence and language teaching. This development has led to the emergence of a new discipline called 'Corpus Linguistic' a term which refers not just to a new computer-based methodology, but as Leech (1992:107) puts it, to a 'new enterprise', a new way of thinking about language, which is challenging some of most deeply rooted ideas about language. Its focus is on performance (rather than competence) description (rather than universal) and quantitative as well as qualitative analysis.

The computer has a key role to play in corpus linguistics. The first important advantage that the computer can offer is that it liberates language analysts 'from drudgery and empowers (them) to focus their creative energies on doing what machines cannot do' (Rundell and Stock, 1992:14). The computer, however, facilitates the automated linguistic analysis which helps in uncovering totally new facts about language. It is this aspect rather than 'the mirroring of intuitive categories of description' (Sinclair, 1986:202), that is the most novel and exciting contribution of corpus linguistics.

3. Analysis of Learner Corpora

One of the advantages of corpus linguistics is that it makes possible earlier. This works on a variety of corpus formats. They work on raw data. A raw corpus of machine readable plain texts (written or spoken) with no extra features added. The corpora can be annotated or unannotated for various linguistic aspects. Leech (1993:275) defines corpus annotation as 'the practice of adding interpretative (especially linguistic) information to an existing corpus of spoken and/or written language by some kind of coding attached, or interpersed with, the electronic representation of the language material itself'. This analysis can be used for the concrete parts-of speech, syntactic, semantic, discoursal and error tagging. A few packages that are available in this area are enlisted at the end of this article.

4. Vocabulary Frequencies in Advanced Learners English

The advent of a corpus of advanced learner English has made possible a new, more concrete approach to the lexical features of learner language. There is a difference of opinion on how learner language actually differs from native speaker language frequently occurs in the literature. This fact is not substantiated by concrete evidence from larger collection of texts until recently. There are some small-scale studies comparing learners of one particular L1 with native speakers. However, for more information we need large numbers of texts of the same type produced by the speakers of many different language groups. When these are compared with each other and with similar native speakers productions a wider perspective can be achieved.

5. Overstatement in Advanced Learners' Writing

Some of the 'advanced' learners are typical in using the writing skills. They are advanced by virtue of having mastered the basic rules of syntax and morphology. Nevertheless, most of them deviate from the norm. The deviations are usually in written production at least concern rather finer points of lexico-grammar and style. These are difficult to point out individually. An attempt can be made to understand their accumulated effect, which tend to generate an impression of 'non-nativeness' of lack of 'idiomaticity.' This aspect of the corpora attempts to identify such peculiarities in learners' intensification of a particular component of the language. In this way, trends become apparent for both native and non-native writing styles and give us a clear idea of both the standard and the learners' progress. This analytical procedure may be laborious but we may learn more about what it means to use English naturally and idiomatically.

6. Learner Corpora : Compiling ELT Dictionaries

The use of learner Corpora is steadily increasing in compiling the ELT dictionaries. In the beginning the emphasis was on the corpora of written native-speaker English. But more recently spoken English and then learners' English becomes the subject of corpus analysis.

The very first dictionary, the New Method English Dictionary of Michael West (1935), drew heavily on the author's pioneering work in 1934 in which he analysed the frequency and meaning of words in a million words of text to produce his General Service List of English Words (1936). The Longman Dictionary of Contemporary English (1979) used citations from the one million-word survey of English Usage, developed by University College, London. By the time the second edition was published in 1987, Longman had developed the 30-million-word Longman Lancaster Corpus (of native-speaker written English), in collaboration with Lancaster University. This corpus establishes the principles that Longman has followed for later corpus development: the importance of balance and representativeness in corpus development.

ELT dictionaries have always tended to be at the forefront of lexicographical development. They have made early use of corpus analysis, they are often the first dictionaries to record new usages; and they take notice of developments in grammatical analysis and grammatical presentation. One reason for their innovation, apart from the need to remain competitive in the market place, is that the target user, the ELT student, has certain specific and recognizable needs. Publishers have to address those needs as effectively as they can.

All the ELT dictionaries now use corpora of native-speaker English to garner information about current usage. The surprising thing is that some of them have been slow to apply the same analysis to the English produced by the learners of English. There have been quite a few books about common learners' errors and inter language errors.

In compiling the dictionaries for learners of English, the lexicographer has to predict what the student would possibly want to know. He should explain that needed aspect in a possible simple manner so that the learner can easily understand. A dictionary is only of use to the student if it includes the word or phrase the students want. The student should easily find them along with the information required by him. The Learners' Corpus can help with each of these stages.

7. Textbook Enhancement: A National Perspective

The presence of persistent errors is detected in the contrastive studies of computerised learner corpora (CLSs). It has been claimed by Granger (1996a) that such findings should be increasingly used in designing new, L1 -sensitive, teaching materials. The computer corpora can be used to design textbook enhancements. The International Corpus of Learner English (ICLE), contains advanced-level argumentative/expository essay writing written in formal, semi-formal, semi-academic style. This process is useful to improve textbook teaching of this type of written English. The assumption is that improved textbook teaching of particular text-type need to be based on solid analysis of corresponding learner data. This kind of product awareness is in line with current developments in ELT and in writing theory, both of which give prominence to the aspects of conventionality in language and language use.

8. Empirically based Computer Assisted Language Learning (CALL)

The research data collected for the purpose of language acquisition can be effectively used in the development of a number of tutorial exercises and this can be used as a tool to assist learners of written English. With the help of learner corpora, the following components can be outlined :

(a) An error recognition (*i.e.*, 'proof reading and editing') exercise intended can be made to sensitive the learners to the most common or most 'serious' errors exposed by the first analysis.

(b) Based on these errors a hyper-text online grammar can be made to give context-sensitive feedback.

(c) The 'underused' lexical and grammatical phrases can be made interactively available to learners from their word processor and

(d) A list-driven concordancer can be developed which interacts with text in these programmes and database.

9. Some Potential Limitations of Computer Corpus.

Research and language acquisition on computer with the aid of learner corpus is too fascinating and sometimes misleading. The entire process seems to be promising but one must be aware of certain limitations mentioned below:

(a) The corpus linguistics generally needs a lot of spade work that is a prerequisite to yield the research results.

(b) The types of linguistic information, which may be practically retrieved from a learner corpus, must be considered. Before the annotation of corpora has taken place, automatic searches are bound to be limited to those features of language, which are easily absorbable in the electronic record of the text.

(c) This process in inevitably encourages the learner and the researcher to put more emphasis on written English than spoken English.

(d) There is a scope for confusion of description and prescription in learner corpus research.

(e) This method of research and language acquisition is uneconomical and tends to become burdensome in Indian context.

LIST OF THE RELATED LINGUISTIC SOFTWARE

Brimingham Taggar (POS Tagger)

Contact http://www.elg.bham.ac.uk.tagger.html

Brill Tagger (POS Tagger)

By anonymous ftp blaze.cs.jhu.edu/pub/brill/programs

CLAWS (POS Tagger)

Contact A. Wilson@ancaster.ac.uk

Correct Grammar (grammar and style checker)

Contact Lifetree Software, 33 New Montgomery Street, Suite 1260, San Francisco, CA 94105, USA

Grammatic (grammar and style checker)

Contact Reference Software International, 330 Townsend Street, Suite 123, San Francisco, CA94107, USA

TACT (text retrieval program)

Contact cch@epas.utoronto.ca

TOSCA analysis environment (POS tagger parser)

Contact tosca@let.kun.nl

TOSCA Tree Editor (syntactic annotation software)

Contact tosca@let.kun.nl

Tuples (recurrent word combination extractor)

Contact mcnery@let.kun.nl

Vocab. Profile (lexical frequency software)

Contact paul.Nation@vuw.ac.nz

Word Cruncher (text retrieval program)

CONTRIBUTORS

P. SHAILAJA, Assistant Professor of English, Kakatiya University, Warangal.

M. RAJESHWAR, Assistant Professor of English, Kakatiya University, Warangal.

G. DAMODAR, Associate Professor of English, Kakatiya University, Warangal.

P. DHANAVEL, Senior Lecturer in English, Tripura University, Agartala.

B. SUDIPTA, Assistant Professor of English, Andhra University, Waltair.

D.S. KESAVA RAO, Senior Lecturer in English, REC, Warangal.

S. THIRUVENKATASWAMI, Lecturer in English, REC, Warangal.

D. SHOBHA, Lecturer in English, Arts & Science College, Andhra Mahila Sabha, OU, Hyderabad.

MALATHY KRISHNAN and INDUMATHY RAMANATHAN, Hyderabad.

M. PRABHAVATHI DEVI, Lecturer in English, YA Govt. College for Women, Chirala.

C. SURYA SREE, Lecturer in English, AP Education Service.

D. VENKAT RAO, Professor of English, CIEFL, Hyderabad.

E. NAGESWARA RAO, formerly Professor of English, OU, Hyderabad.

SUDHANSHU RANJAN, Door Darshan Kendra, Patna.

TECLE GHEBREMUSE, Head, Department of English, University of Asmara, Eritrea.

V.D. SINGH, Professor of English, CIEFL, Hyderabad.

C.B. SHARMA, Lecturer in English, JM Patel College, Bhandara, Maharashtra.

C. GOVERDHAN, Jr. Lecturer in English, Govt. Junior College, Nirmal.

KESARAJ KUMAR, Assistant Professor of English, Kakatiya University, Warangal. AP.

R. SUBHASHINI, Lecturer in English, Warangal, AP.